CONTENTS

INTRODUCTION

The Wallace Collection is a national museum that displays the art collections brought together by the first four marquesses of Hertford and Sir Richard Wallace, the likely illegitimate son of the 4th Marquess of Hertford. It was bequeathed to the British nation by Lady Wallace, Sir Richard's widow, in 1897.

Among the Collection's treasures are an outstanding array of 18th-century French art, many important 17th- and 19th-century paintings, medieval and Renaissance works of art and one of the finest collections of princely arms and armour in the United Kingdom.

The Collection is displayed at Hertford House, formerly the principal London residence of the marquesses of Hertford and Sir Richard and Lady Wallace. It was opened to the public as a museum in 1900.

Hertford House, about 1812–13.

HERTFORD HOUSE

The Seymour-Conway family's association with Hertford House began in 1797, when the 2nd Marquess of Hertford took up residence there. The 2nd Marchioness was a great hostess, and in the first decades of the 19th century, Hertford House was much visited by fashionable London society. The 3rd Marquess of Hertford preferred to live at his other London residences, Dorchester House and St Dunstan's Villa, and the 4th Marquess of Hertford, who lived most of his life in Paris, used the building largely as a store for his ever-expanding art collection. The 4th Marquess of Hertford died in 1870 and Richard Wallace took over the lease of Hertford House from the 5th Marquess of Hertford the following year. Wallace, who had been brought up in Paris by his likely father and grandmother, moved into Hertford House in 1875 only after extensive alterations to the building had been carried out.

He died in Paris in 1890, but his widow continued to live at Hertford House, aided by their secretary, John Murray Scott, until her death in 1897. Between 1897 and 1900, the former private residence was converted into a public museum. Galleries replaced the stabling, coach houses and smoking room, as well as some private rooms on the first floor. Many substantial changes have been made since the museum opened in order to make it a welcoming place for successive generations of visitors.

THE FOUNDERS

Although some important works of art now in the Collection were acquired in the 18th century by the 1st and 2nd Marquesses of Hertford (for example, some paintings by Giovanni Antonio Canal, called Canaletto, and Joshua Reynolds), the first member of the family to show a real interest in art was the 3rd Marquess of Hertford. A friend of the Prince Regent, later George IV of the United Kingdom, he acquired important 17th-century Dutch paintings, French furniture, gilt bronzes and Sèvres porcelain.

However, it was his son, the 4th Marquess of Hertford, one of the greatest collectors of the 19th century, who determined the essential character of the Collection we see today. Brought up in Paris by his mother after she separated from his father, the 4th Marquess of Hertford later lived in style in a large apartment in the rue Laffitte and at Bagatelle, a château in the Bois de Boulogne. His art collecting combined aspects of both French and English taste and his enormous wealth (gained largely from estates in England and in particular Ireland) enabled him to indulge that taste to the full. His acquisitions included the great majority of the paintings, porcelain and furniture now in the museum, as well as the non-European arms and armour. He bought art on such a large scale that much of his collection was kept in storage rather than on display, though he was an important lender to contemporary exhibitions.

The 4th Marquess of Hertford never married. After spending his earliest years in London, Richard Wallace became his likely father's assistant and adviser in Paris, particularly in matters relating to art. In 1870, he inherited the 4th Marquess of Hertford's unentailed collection and property in France, England and Ireland. A great philanthropist, Wallace was made a baronet in 1871 for his charitable services during the Siege of Paris, which took place during the Franco-Prussian War (1870–71). Before leaving Paris, he presented the city with fifty cast-iron fountains, known as 'Les Wallaces', which provided free, clean drinking water to the public. In 1872, he brought over to London many of the works of art inherited from the 4th Marquess of Hertford, to which he added important collections of medieval and Renaissance objects and European arms and armour. While Hertford House was being converted to accommodate his collection (1872–5), Wallace's loan of more than 2,000 works of art as the opening exhibition of the Bethnal Green Museum in the East End of London was a popular sensation. In 1890, he bequeathed his property to his widow, Lady Wallace, born Julie Amélie Charlotte Castelnau, who, on her death seven years later, left the works of art on the ground and first floors of Hertford House to the British nation. She left most of the rest of her property, which included many fine works of art, to her secretary, John Murray Scott.

Richard Seymour-Conway, 4th Marquess of Hertford, about 1860.

Sir Richard Wallace in the Great Gallery at Hertford House, late 1870s–mid-1880s.

Lady Wallace, probably early 1890s.

THE SEYMOUR-CONWAY FAMILY

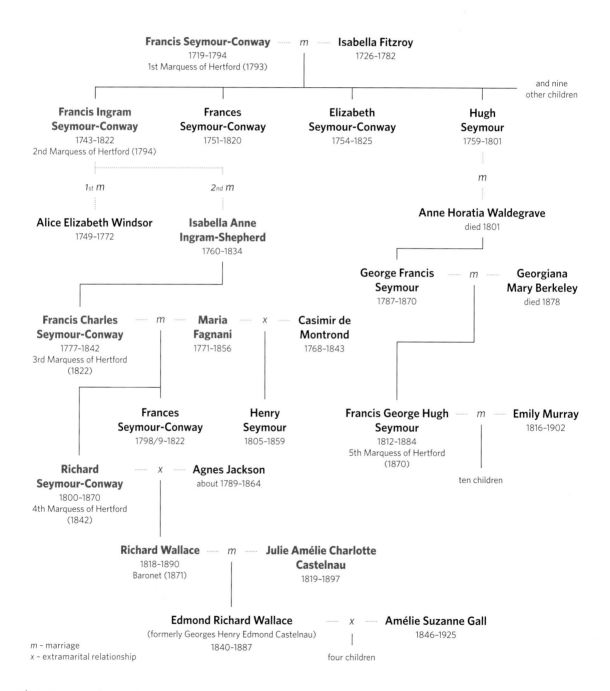

Francis Seymour-Conway ---- *m* ---- **Isabella Fitzroy**
1719–1794 / 1726–1782
1st Marquess of Hertford (1793)

and nine other children

Francis Ingram Seymour-Conway
1743–1822
2nd Marquess of Hertford (1794)

Frances Seymour-Conway
1751–1820

Elizabeth Seymour-Conway
1754–1825

Hugh Seymour
1759–1801

1st m

2nd m

m

Alice Elizabeth Windsor
1749–1772

Isabella Anne Ingram-Shepherd
1760–1834

Anne Horatia Waldegrave
died 1801

George Francis Seymour
1787–1870

m

Georgiana Mary Berkeley
died 1878

Francis Charles Seymour-Conway
1777–1842
3rd Marquess of Hertford (1822)

m

Maria Fagnani
1771–1856

x

Casimir de Montrond
1768–1843

Frances Seymour-Conway
1798/9–1822

Henry Seymour
1805–1859

Francis George Hugh Seymour
1812–1884
5th Marquess of Hertford (1870)

m

Emily Murray
1816–1902

Richard Seymour-Conway
1800–1870
4th Marquess of Hertford (1842)

x

Agnes Jackson
about 1789–1864

ten children

Richard Wallace
1818–1890
Baronet (1871)

m

Julie Amélie Charlotte Castelnau
1819–1897

Edmond Richard Wallace
(formerly Georges Henry Edmond Castelnau)
1840–1887

x

Amélie Suzanne Gall
1846–1925

four children

m – marriage
x – extramarital relationship

THE COLLECTION

ENTRANCE HALL

The Entrance Hall has retained the aspect it had in Sir Richard and Lady Wallace's day more than any other interior in the building. Coming into this space, the eye is immediately drawn to the Grand Staircase, with its splendid French wrought-iron balustrade. Made for a staircase in John Law's Royal Bank in Paris in 1719–20, it is lavishly decorated with royal emblems of sunflowers and what may be interlaced *L*s for Louis XV of France or *J*s and *L*s for John Law, as well as cornucopias of coins, banknotes and fruit. Sir Richard bought it about 1871, following its dismantling, and had it enlarged to fit the double staircase at Hertford House, where it was installed in 1874.

The Entrance Hall, about 1890.

F362

Pair of vases and covers, about 1684

Giovanni Battista Pozzi (active in the late 17th century)
H. 72.5 cm | Inv. nos F362–3

During the 17th century, a fashion developed among French collectors for hardstone vases, and for hardstone works of art more generally. Some of these prized objects were made in ancient Rome, where marble and porphyry were used extensively, or were carved from architectural fragments that were found in the city in the 17th century. This pair of vases was presumably carved from old porphyry by Pozzi in Rome in the 1680s. They were commissioned by Matthieu de la Teulière, the director of the French Academy in Rome, and displayed by Louis XIV of France in the Hall of Mirrors at the Palace of Versailles.

Busts of a Woman and Man, about 1650

Rome, Italy
H. 72 cm (S18) and
H. 69.2 cm (S17) |
Inv. nos S18 and S17

These marble busts show a young woman with her hair tied up, wearing a tunic and a headdress to which a posy of flowers is attached, and a man with closely cropped hair, wearing similar dress. The woman is full of elegance and dignity, and her allure is enhanced through her direct but slightly dreamy stare, while the man is alert and lively, turning and smiling as if he is about to speak. They are realistic portraits with a strong sense of individuality rather than the more common 17th-century busts of Black people, which emphasise the heroic or idealised and do not attempt to portray real people. Sadly, the identity of the sculptor and the sitters has not yet been established.

Landseer was the most fashionable and successful painter of the early Victorian period; his work was much admired by Queen Victoria herself. This painting is a rare instance of Landseer responding to the contemporary interest in the Middle East and its cultures: an Arab mare and her foal rest on carpets inside a tent, with two Persian greyhounds and two monkeys (one wearing an earring). Their owner's presence is suggested by the two pipes in the jar on the right.

The Arab Tent, about 1865–6

Edwin Landseer (1802–1873)

H. 153.6 x W. 226.4 cm | Inv. no. P376

Staircase balustrade, 1719–20

France

H. 0.9 m | Inv. no. F68

Installed on the main staircase of Hertford House by Sir Richard Wallace in 1874, this balustrade was originally in the Hôtel de Nevers in Paris when it was occupied by the Royal Bank. The cornucopias overflowing with coins and banknotes are suggestive of the new monetary system proposed by John Law, who persuaded the regent of France, the duc d'Orléans, to establish in 1716 a national bank capable of issuing notes. The central decorative motif may be derived from Law's cipher, JL, or may recall the interlaced Ls of Louis XV of France. The balustrade was much altered for its insertion into Hertford House, but it remains the finest example of iron- and brasswork from the French Regency period (1715–23) to have survived.

FRONT STATE ROOM

THE GRAND LONDON TOWNHOUSE

This room reveals the opulence of the grand London townhouse in the 1870s and sets the scene for visitors to the Collection. The State Rooms were the grandest rooms in the house, in which the most important visitors were received.

When Hertford House was the home of Sir Richard and Lady Wallace, the Front State Room was, as now, hung with portraits. Some of the modern furniture seen in the photograph below is no longer in the Collection, but the mounted porcelain displayed on the cabinets and the superb chandelier made by Jacques Caffiéri have been returned to the room.

The Front State Room, about 1890.

Queen Victoria, **1838**
Thomas Sully (1783–1872)
H. 142.5 x W. 112.5 cm | Inv. no. P564

In 1837, the English-born American artist Sully visited London, bringing with him a commission from the American Society of the Sons of St George (an English patriotic society) to paint a portrait of the new queen, Victoria. During five sittings at Buckingham Palace, Sully painted a bust-length study, and from this he derived the full-length version, now in a private collection, for the Sons of St George. The Collection's painting, also based on the life study, was commissioned for an engraving by Charles Edward Wagstaff. Principally through this engraving, it became one of the best-known images of the young Queen Victoria.

Margaret, Countess of Blessington, **about 1821–2**
Thomas Lawrence (1769–1830)
H. 91.5 x W. 67 cm | Inv. no. P558

This portrait is one of the best examples of Lawrence's skill in combining precise detail with a loose handling of paint. The sitter is Margaret Power, Countess of Blessington, who was a renowned novelist, literary editor and host of a salon at Gore House in Kensington. She is dressed very simply and wears little jewellery. The only indication of her aristocratic status is the ermine-trimmed robe draped over the chair. According to Lord Byron, the painting 'set all London raving' when it was exhibited at the Royal Academy in 1822.

Two ice-cream coolers, 1778

Sèvres Manufactory
H. 23.2 cm (C476) and H. 25.2 cm (C477) | Inv. nos C476–7

These coolers, part of a group of four in the Collection, come from a service made for Catherine II of Russia. The service contained 797 pieces and was sent to Russia in June 1779. It comprised dinner, dessert, tea and coffee services for sixty guests, as well as a centrepiece, making it one of the most extravagant commissions received by Sèvres in the 18th century. Although the original metal liners for ice-cream have been lost, their function can be recognised by the gilded icicles and fountains on the covers. The 4th Marquess of Hertford acquired these and many other pieces after they were looted from the Winter Palace in St Petersburg during a fire in 1837. The other pieces were returned to Russia by Hertford through the dealer John Webb in 1857.

Lady Hamilton as a Bacchante, 1803
Henry Bone (1755–1834), after Élisabeth-Louise Vigée Le Brun (1755–1842)
H. 22.2 x W. 28 cm | Inv. no. M21

Bone was appointed enamel painter to George III, George IV and William IV of the United Kingdom, and achieved extraordinary financial success with his copies in enamel after old master paintings. This enamel is after an oil painting by the French artist Vigée Le Brun. It shows Emma, Lady Hamilton, the famous wife of Sir William Hamilton, British envoy to Naples, and mistress of the great naval hero Vice Admiral Nelson. The original, now in a private collection, was painted in 1790. Bone's copy was commissioned by Sir William and bequeathed by him to Nelson the year it was painted.

BACK STATE ROOM

THE ROCOCO AT THE TIME OF LOUIS XV OF FRANCE AND MADAME DE POMPADOUR

The Back State Room is today dedicated to the patronage of Louis XV of France and his longtime lover, friend, advisor and confidante, Madame de Pompadour. It displays some of the greatest examples in the Collection of art in the Rococo style, which flourished under their auspices. 'Rococo' derives from the French word 'rocaille', meaning loose stones or rocky ground. This exuberant, animated style explores asymmetrical natural shapes with fountain imagery, foliage and flowers, swirling scrolls and sea animals.

Sir Richard and Lady Wallace used the Back State Room to entertain guests at Hertford House. During their lifetime, it had wooden panelling on the walls; the great chandelier by Jacques Caffiéri remains in the room.

The Back State Room, about 1890.

Flowers on a Fountain with a
***Peacock,* about 1700–10**

Jan Weenix (1642–1719)
H. 177 x W. 165 cm | Inv. no. P59

The most spectacular of a group of thirteen paintings by Weenix in the Collection, this painting is a particularly fine and characteristic example of his late style. Weenix combined natural and architectural elements, composed in the grand manner, with dramatic lighting to obtain a monumental effect. The translucent bloom of the grapes, the curling leaves, the pomegranate splitting with ripeness, the peacock's convincingly rendered feathers and the confident modelling of the stone sculptures demonstrate Weenix's exquisite ability to create different textures in paint. A plethora of details, such as the snail on the stone ledge, provide variety and visual interest.

Garniture of three vases, 1758

Sèvres Manufactory

H. 38.1 cm (C248), H. 39.3 cm (C249) and
H. 38.8 cm (C250) | Inv. nos C248–50

This exquisite garniture consists of two vases
with elephants' heads supporting candleholders
and a boat-shaped pot-pourri vase. Conceived by
chief designer Jean-Claude Duplessis the Elder,
they are among the finest examples of the unique
craftsmanship and stylistic extravagance Sèvres
had reached by the mid-1750s. The piercings on the
neck of the vase were required for the perfume to
permeate and are a complex decorative pattern of
entwining scrolls, while the cover is decorated with
naturalistically sculpted and painted flowers. The
inventories of Madame de Pompadour's apartments
at the Palace of Versailles and her Parisian
townhouse list three vases whose description closely
matches this garniture in the Collection. She might
have bought this set in 1759 and then displayed the
vases in different houses.

The Dead Roe and **The Dead Wolf,** 1721

Jean-Baptiste Oudry
(1686–1755)
H. 193 x W. 260 cm |
Inv. nos P630 and
P626

These are early works by the French painter Oudry. They were likely inserted directly into the wooden panelling of a dining room. It is fitting, therefore, that references to gastronomy abound in the form of signifiers of the aristocratic privilege of the hunt in *The Dead Roe* and the remains of an elegant picnic in *The Dead Wolf.* Oudry was known for his humane and moving portraits of animal subjects. His empathetic approach is conveyed by the dog, who looks soulfully out at the viewer from the left side of *The Dead Roe.*

Astronomical clock, about 1750

Movement designed by Alexandre Fortier (about 1700–1770) and made by Michel Stollewerck (died 1768)
H. 294.5 cm | Inv. no. F98

Probably made for Jean Paris de Monmartel, banker to the French court (and godfather of Madame de Pompadour), this monumental clock was in its time at the cutting edge of science, being able to show both solar and mean time, the time in any part of the northern hemisphere, the day and date of the month, the sign of the Zodiac and the times of the rising and setting of the sun and moon. The clock's mechanisms are housed in an extravagant case, veneered with purplewood and other woods and mounted with gilt bronze. Surmounting the clock face at the top is Love triumphing over Time, a sculptural group in patinated bronze that had been a popular decorative feature of clocks since the early 18th century.

Inkstand, 1759

Sèvres Manufactory
H. 17 cm | Inv. no. C488

Designed by Jean-Claude Duplessis the Elder, this is perhaps the most important piece by Sèvres in the Collection. It was given by Louis XV of France to his daughter, Madame Adélaïde. Two medallions reveal this: one in the centre of the tray shows the head of Louis XV, and another at one end bears the cipher *MA* (for Marie-Adélaïde). The terrestrial globe on the right contained an inkwell, and the celestial globe on the left (with the signs of the Zodiac and piercings for stars) contained a silver-gilt sand shaker. Inside the cushion was a sponge for Madame Adélaïde to wipe her pen, and inside the crown of France was a bell for her to ring when she wanted her maid to collect the letter she had written.

This superb rococo chest-of-drawers was made for Louis XV of France's bedchamber at the Palace of Versailles, and it has the stamp of the palace (crossed Vs) on the back. The carcase is made from oak, veneered with kingwood and bloodwood imported from South America. The veneers have faded but once formed a strong pattern in vibrant purple-brown and deep pink. The gilt-bronze mounts twist and turn wildly in the form of leaves and rock formations all over the front and sides of the chest-of-drawers. Such mounts would have helped to light a room in the evenings by reflecting candlelight.

Chest-of-drawers, 1739

Antoine-Robert Gaudreaus (1682–1746), gilt-bronze mounts by Jacques Caffiéri (1678–1755)
H. 88.8 cm | Inv. no. F86

Chandelier, 1751

Jacques Caffiéri (1678–1755) and probably Philippe Caffiéri (1714–1774)
H. 179 cm | Inv. no. F83

Like the smaller nine-light chandelier in the Front State Room, this magnifcent twelve-light chandelier was made by Jacques Caffiéri, probably assisted by his elder son, Philippe. With its flowing S-shaped arms and exuberant motifs, the chandelier is a prime example of the Rococo style. It was almost certainly given by Louis XV of France to his eldest daughter, Louise-Élisabeth, Duchess of Parma, during one of her visits to Paris in the 1750s. In 1803, it was hanging in the grand salon of the duchess's former palace in Colorno, Italy. Unusually for a work in gilt bronze, the chandelier is signed with the engraved mark of Caffiéri and dated 1751.

Ewer and basin, 1731–2 and later

France, gold mounts by Jean
Gaillard (active 1695–1754)
H. 18.9 cm (ewer) | Inv. no. W198

The rock crystal used for this ewer
and basin is exceptionally clear. The
set, especially the hollow form of
the ewer, would have taken great
skill to make. The gold mounts of
the ewer include a handle in the
form of a young Triton wrestling
with a snake-like sea monster and
a knob on the cover in the shape of
a barking dog. Three examples are
known (only two with their basins).
This set belonged to Madame de
Pompadour.

Pot-pourri vase and cover, about 1761

Sèvres Manufactory
H. 44.1 cm | Inv. no. C256

This spectacular piece is the last and most
elaborate of three ship-shaped vase models
created during the 1750s at Sèvres by Jean-
Claude Duplessis the Elder. Resting on a
wave-patterned foot, its 'portholes' on the
shoulder, figureheads with bowsprits on
the sides and the sails, ropes and pennon
on the cover are a playful take on the ship
theme. The complex piercings on the cover
are not only decorative but also highly
functional: intended as a pot-pourri vase to
be filled with perfumed flowers, herbs and
spices, the openings would have allowed
the perfume to circulate. Decorated with
underglaze blue and overglaze green
ground colours and richly varied gilding,
the vase shows birds in landscapes painted
on both sides.

DINING ROOM

18TH-CENTURY STILL LIFES AND PORTRAITS

This room contains works of French 18th-century portraiture by Jean-Antoine Houdon and Jean-Marc Nattier, as we all as two oil sketches by Jean-François de Troy for the decoration of Louis XV of France's dining room at the Palace of Fontainebleau, which were shown to the king for approval.

As its name suggests, the Dining Room was the formal room in which Sir Richard and Lady Wallace would generally take meals with invited guests or on special occasions.

The Dining Room, about 1888.

A Hunt Breakfast and *The Death of a Stag,* 1737

Jean-François de Troy (1679–1752)
H. 54.7 x W. 44.8 cm (P463) and H.
54.5 x W. 45 cm (P470) | Inv. nos P463
and P470

These are preparatory oil sketches for paintings commissioned to decorate Louis XV of France's dining room at the Palace of Fontainebleau. *A Hunt Breakfast* depicts the gathering before the hunt, underlining the essentially gallant nature of the gathering through the conversational attitudes of the male and female figures, while *The Death of a Stag* depicts a stag's final moments as it is hunted by a group of dogs and figures in woodland. The paintings are remarkable for their fluid, rapid handling and vivid colouring, recalling the influence of Peter Paul Rubens and Venetian art on French painting at the beginning of the 18th century.

Chest-of-drawers, 1782 (veneer later)

Jean-Henri Riesener (1732–1806), gilt-bronze mounts
gilded by François Rémond (1747–1812)
H. 88.5 cm | Inv. no. F248

In March 1782, Marie-Antoinette had two chests-of-drawers delivered to her newly decorated apartment at the Château de Marly, which were recorded in her bedroom. This is believed to be one of them but looks very different from when Riesener delivered it. It has been reveneered with mahogany, rather than the trellis marquetry used regularly by Riesener on his royal furniture. The gilt-bronze mounts are particularly beautiful and very much to Marie-Antoinette's taste. There was once a gilt-bronze frame encircling a marquetry medallion on the front.

Madame de Sérilly, 1782

Jean-Antoine Houdon (1741–1828)
H. 62 cm | Inv. no. S26

Madame de Sérilly was a well-educated socialite, famed for her beauty. At the time this bust was sculpted, she and her husband, who was treasurer-general in the war ministry, lived in a splendid house in the fashionable Marais district of Paris. In 1794, during the height of the French Revolution, the couple was arrested. Sérilly's husband was executed, while she was spared only because she claimed to be pregnant. After two further tragic marriages, she died in 1799 at the age of thirty-six. Houdon, the leading French sculptor of his time, was renowned for his portrait busts. This superb example was exhibited at the Paris Salon of 1783.

BILLIARD ROOM

THE ARTS UNDER LOUIS XIV OF FRANCE

The Billiard Room is a showcase for some of the best furniture by André-Charles Boulle and for the arts under Louis XIV of France and during the subsequent years of the French Regency (1715–23), which saw the duc d'Orléans rule on behalf of the young Louis XV. Boulle was cabinetmaker to Louis XIV, the self-styled Sun King, during whose reign France became pre-eminent in the arts. Louis XIV set up a well-organised and efficient system of state support for the arts to create the official image of the monarchy and to support the economy.

When Sir Richard and Lady Wallace lived at Hertford House, the Billiard Room was dominated by a huge billiard table, as was usual in many large houses at the time.

The Billiard Room, about 1888.

Cabinet on stand, about 1670–75

Attributed to André-Charles Boulle (1642–1732)

H. 186.7 cm | Inv. no. F16

Dated to the early 1670s, this spectacular cabinet was made at a time when Boulle was building his reputation and had just been appointed cabinetmaker to Louis XIV of France. Only four other similar cabinets are known to exist. The naturalistic depiction of flowers and insects in the wood marquetry reflects the popularity of Dutch still-life painting in the last few decades of the 17th century. This is combined with more imaginary elements of baroque architecture. The medal of Louis XIV at the front of the cabinet reflects the interest in medals among French art collectors at the time and may indicate that the drawers in the cabinet were used to store small, precious objects. Such cabinets were, however, made largely to impress.

These sculptures depict Jupiter and Juno in scenes that illustrate the myth of the creation of the world. The Titans sought to challenge the gods but Jupiter crushed them with his thunderbolts. From their blood a new race of evil men was created. Jupiter decided to extinguish the corrupt race by unleashing a flood that would cover the whole earth. Juno assisted him with the imprisonment of three of the Winds, so that the South Wind could create a great storm and flood unhindered. Probably cast in Rome after models made by Algardi for Philip IV of Spain, they later entered the French royal collection.

Jupiter Victorious over the Titans: Fire and *Juno Controlling the Winds: Air*, **about 1650–54, cast probably Rome, about 1655–81**

Alessandro Algardi (1598–1654)

H. 126.9 cm (S161) and H. 125.1 cm (S162) | Inv. nos S161–2

Charles Le Brun, about 1676

Antoine Coysevox (1640–1720)
H. 66 cm | Inv. no. S60

This bust of the great artist Charles Le Brun was exhibited before the French Academy in 1676, serving as the model for a marble version (now in the Musée du Louvre, Paris) that Coysevox offered to the Academy as his reception piece in 1679. Le Brun was not only first painter to Louis XIV of France but also chancellor of the Academy and, as head of the Gobelins Manufactory, the leader of a team producing luxury furnishings unsurpassed in Europe. Coysevox rose to become one of the greatest sculptors of his time and, from 1678, was much employed at the Palace of Versailles. He shows Le Brun in his day shirt, with only a miniature of Louis XIV, tucked within his cloak, hinting at his position and status.

Mademoiselle de Clermont en sultane, 1733

Jean-Marc Nattier (1685–1766)
H. 109 x W. 104.5 cm | Inv. no. P456

Mademoiselle de Clermont, a member of the extended French royal family, has been depicted as a sultana in this painting by Nattier in an early work of *turquerie*. Clermont is shown undressed in a harem, which was construed as an erotically charged space in the Western imagination. The setting also provided the rationale for the representation of Black attendants. The identity of these women is unknown today, nor is it clear whether Nattier worked after live models. However, the painting was made only several decades after the establishment of the *Code Noir*, which codified slavery in the French empire. Therefore, it is likely that the women represented here were understood by contemporary viewers to be enslaved. Their presence in relation to Clermont would have reinforced a sense of her wealth and status.

Madame de Ventadour with Louis XIV and his Heirs, 1715–20

French School
H. 127.6 x W. 161 cm | Inv. no. P122

This picture was painted to celebrate the role of the duchesse de Ventadour in ensuring the continuation of the Bourbon dynasty in France. She is shown alongside her little charge, the duc d'Anjou, future Louis XV, whom she saved during the measles epidemic of 1712. They are surrounded by his ancestors: Henri IV, represented in a bust on the left; Louis XIII in a bust on the right; Louis XIV in the centre of the picture; and Louis, the Grand Dauphin, leaning against his father's chair. On the right stands Louis XIV's grandson and the duc d'Anjou's father, the duc de Bourgogne. The wealth and power of the dynasty is underlined by the palatial setting, which evokes the Palace of Versailles and its imagery of the god Apollo.

Pair of lacquer cabinets, about 1680

Japan (Kyoto?) and France
H. 86 cm (excluding feet) |
Inv. nos F18–19

Japanese lacquer was enormously prized in Europe in the 17th and 18th centuries. This pair of cabinets belongs to a type of Japanese cabinet made for export, though it is of higher quality than most export lacquer. There are ten drawers inside, each with a lacquer front. Some decorative elements of the exterior, such as the mountains, rocks and roofs of buildings, are raised in low relief, and the summit of Mount Fuji has applied silver leaf to represent snow. The gilt-bronze feet were made in France in the late 17th century.

16TH-CENTURY GALLERY

THE COLLECTOR'S CABINET

The 16th-Century Gallery houses works of art from the medieval and Renaissance periods and a group of important Renaissance paintings. This part of the Collection was mainly assembled by Sir Richard Wallace, who, like many 19th-century collectors, was fascinated by the art and history of Europe during the Middle Ages and Renaissance.

The 16th-Century Gallery was divided into two smaller rooms during Sir Richard and Lady Wallace's lifetime. The contemporary photograph below shows how one room was arranged by Sir Richard as an art cabinet (known as a *Kunstkammer*), with paintings and ceramics densely hung on the walls and smaller works of art kept in cases or inside Renaissance cabinets. The other room connected with the Front State Room and was known as the Canaletto Room for its ensemble of *vedute*, or topographical view paintings showing Venetian cityscapes.

The 16th-Century Gallery, about 1888.

Sir Richard Leveson, about 1595–1600

Isaac Oliver (1558–1617)

H. 5.1 x W. 4 cm | Inv. no. M287

Oliver, a prominent member of the artistic community of Elizabethan and Jacobean London, was the most important pupil of the miniaturist Nicholas Hilliard, whose success he threatened towards the end of the 16th century. This miniature reveals his refined and cosmopolitan manner in details such as the wavy brown hair and carefully drawn face. The sitter was a naval commander, who served on the Ark Royal against the Spanish Armada in 1588 and was eventually appointed vice admiral of England in 1604.

An Allegory of True Love, about 1547

Pieter Pourbus (1523–1584)

H. 132.8 x W. 205.7 cm | Inv. no. P531

Pourbus's masterpiece depicts a group of mythological and allegorical characters. In the centre of the painting is an older man, Sapiens (Wisdom), who embraces Fidutia (Fidelity). She offers the wise man spiritual love sanctified by Christian matrimony, while the other figures warn the viewer of the folly of carnal love. The complex subject reflects Pourbus's involvement with the erudite circles of the Bruges chambers of rhetoric (literary societies), while the elegant figures reveal his debt to Italian Mannerism. The lively landscape background and naturalistic detail also demonstrate the development of naturalism in painting in the southern Netherlands.

The Good Shepherd, about 1600

Sri Lanka or India (Goa)
H. 12.8 cm | Inv. no. S50

This figure shows Christ as the Good Shepherd, symbolising his care for and guidance of his flock. It belongs to a small group of rock crystal figures of the Christ Child produced in Goa and Ceylon (present-day Sri Lanka). This Christian theme was introduced there by missionaries, who accompanied Portuguese traders. Similar statues in ivory are known. The figure is a superb example of the local tradition of carving rock crystal and decorating it with gold and precious stones.

Seated woman, about 1480–90

Giovanni Fonduli da Crema (active 1460s, died before 1497)
H. 20.5 cm | Inv. no. S72

This sculpture is considered the finest early Renaissance bronze in the Collection. The source for its composition is a classical sculpture of a seated nymph putting on her sandal. The finely chiselled hair and hands, the sensuous curves and polished surfaces of the body and the tantalising contrast of textures and colours of the Collection's sculpture would have made it a treasured object in any collector's cabinet in Renaissance Italy. It is unusual in its extensive application of gilding. Fonduli da Crema, who was active in Padua, was obviously proud of his achievement. Unusually, he included a signature in a prominent place: a cartouche at the back of the seat. This makes it one of very few signed bronzes that may be dated before 1500.

Initial 'A' with Galeazzo Maria Sforza in prayer, probably 1477

Cristoforo de Predis (active 1470s)
H. 22.4 x W. 18.9 cm (initial) and H. 9.7 x W. 22.8 cm (border) | Inv. no. M342

The initial 'A', perhaps cut from a choir book, shows Galeazzo Maria Sforza, Duke of Milan, a famously martial figure, kneeling in prayer to God, presumably asking for victory in the battle taking place in the middle distance. The arms of the dukes of Milan are enclosed in a wreath in the border. The battle depicted probably took place during the campaigns of 1476, during which Sforza fought against the armies sent into northern Italy by Charles the Bold, Duke of Burgundy. Below the initial is the artist's signature, partly rubbed out: *Opus Xpstofori de Predis VII die Aprilis 147[-]*. Cristoforo, brother of the better-known Ambrogio, signed various manuscripts in the 1470s.

The Virgin and Child with the Infant Baptist, about 1517–19

Andrea del Sarto (1486–1530)
H. 106.5 x W. 81.3 cm | Inv. no. P9

The Virgin supports the standing Christ, who, with his outstretched right hand, blesses the infant St John the Baptist at the lower left. St John is already dressed in animal skins of the kind he will wear when preaching in the desert. Behind him are two angels. In the landscape to the right, St Francis kneels before an angel playing a viol. The painting demonstrates Del Sarto's increasingly mannerist elegance in its colouring, complex artificial composition and elegantly refined poses, which nevertheless convey emotion with great immediacy. Numerous related versions and copies attest to the popularity of the composition.

Platter: *Apollo and the Muses*, about 1580

Martial Courteys

L. 56.7 cm | Inv. no. C595

In classical mythology, Mount Parnassus in Greece was sacred to the Olympian god Apollo, who was associated with musical harmony, and his companions, the nine Muses, goddesses of creative inspiration. Here, the *lira da braccio*-playing god Apollo presides over the music-making Muses, while behind them two poets crowned with laurel wreaths converse. The winged horse Pegasus stamps to prevent the mountain from rising in response to the music. His stamping creates the Hippocrene stream, personified by the young woman below Apollo, who pours water from a vase. The composition derives ultimately from a lost preparatory study for Raffaello Santi's (called Raphael) *Parnassus* fresco in the Vatican. However, its direct source is an engraving after a drawing by Luca Penni.

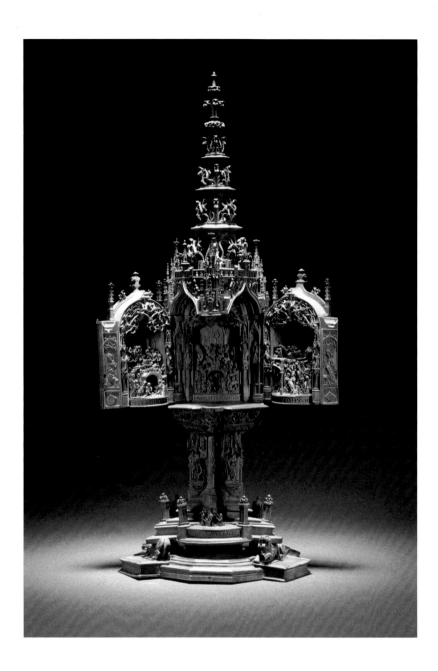

The Adoration of the Magi, **about 1500–30**

Adam Dircksz and workshop (active about 1500–30)
H. 43.8 cm | Inv. no. S279

The intricacy of miniature boxwood carvings made in the Netherlands has always been a source of wonder. Intended for personal devotion, they quickly became desirable collectors' objects. This miniature gothic altarpiece, which is made of three panels, is richly carved with scenes from the Old and New Testaments, with the Adoration of the Magi in the centre. A kneeling couple in the panels on the far left and right probably depicts those who commissioned the piece. Their identity remains unknown, although the man is accompanied by St Nicholas, which may be a clue that they shared the same name.

Charles IX, King of France, about 1570–79

Germain Pilon (about 1525–1590)
H. 70.9 cm | Inv. no. S154

Charles IX acceded to the throne of France at the age of ten. Weak in health, he was largely under the sway of his mother, Catherine de' Medici, and the duc de Guise, the leader of the Catholic faction at a time of intense religious strife in France. The notorious St Bartholomew's Day massacre of the French Huguenots happened during his reign. For all the splendour of Charles's costume, with his laurel crown and military armour, the thin lips and suspicious eyes of this masterful portrait brilliantly suggest the young king's brittle and nervous character. It is one of the finest surviving works of Pilon, who was appointed sculptor to both Charles IX and his successor, Henri III.

Baby-linen basket, about 1650–1700

Lucas Luicksen (active 1652–77)
L. 63.5 cm | Inv. no. W163

This silver basket was used for a new-born child's layette, which consisted of nappies, clothes and a christening dress. Baby-linen baskets were usually made of cane. However, the richest Dutch families owned baskets made of silver. Only seven baby-linen baskets made in the Netherlands are known to survive, all dating from the 17th century. This example bears the marks of the town of Deventer and the silversmith Luicksen. The relief in the centre depicts the fleeing nymph Daphne being turned into a laurel tree to escape the attentions of the god Apollo. It derives from a design by the celebrated Utrecht silversmith Paulus van Vianen.

Beaker, 1609

Probably Bohemia (Czech Republic)
H. 28.3 cm | Inv. no. C563

Known as a *Humpen*, this type of enamelled
drinking glass was a popular vessel for use at
festive gatherings in Bohemia and Germany.
The *Humpen* was one of the most abundantly
produced types of enamelled glass in 17th-
century Bohemia and Germany. They were at
their most popular from the 1570s until well into
the 17th century and numerous examples have
survived. Many originally had covers, but these
have often been lost or broken. Drinking scenes
were a popular subject for enamellers of German
and Bohemian glass. There was a tradition of
welcoming guests by presenting them with a
capacious drinking cup or tankard. This beaker
is a *Willkomm*, a category of *Humpen* specifically
intended to be used for welcoming guests.

The Bell Shrine of St Mura, 11th–16th centuries (decoration applied in stages)

Ireland
H. 15.5 cm | Inv. no. W2

This bronze hand bell is reputed to have belonged
to St Mura, the first abbot of the Abbey of
Fahan in County Donegal, Ireland. The bell was
believed to have the power to alleviate suffering,
especially in childbirth. For centuries, the care
of Irish relics was entrusted to designated
families called 'keepers'. The last keeper of this
bell was a poor fisherman, who sold it in the
1840s. Sir Richard Wallace bought it in 1879 and
must have appreciated not only the historical
and artistic qualities of the object but also its
Irish provenance. He owned large estates in
County Antrim and took his responsibilities as a
landowner very seriously, becoming the principal
benefactor of the city of Lisburn.

Goblet, about 1500

Venice, Italy
H. 18 cm | Inv. no. C513

This masterpiece from the 'Golden Age' of Venetian glassmaking is an exceptional example of the glassmakers' ability to simulate hardstones. The external striated decoration imitates chalcedony in contrasting warm and cold palettes, while the inside of the bowl may simulate jade. A writer of the period provides us with a sense of the awe in which this kind of work was held, proclaiming: 'There is no kind of precious stone that cannot be imitated by the industry of the glassworkers, a sweet contest of nature and man'. The goblet's shape is inspired by contemporary metalwork, and it may originally have had a cover. Prestigious glass goblets of similar form were made in imitation of rock crystal and turquoise.

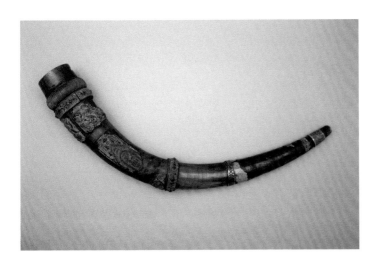

Horn of St Hubert, second half of the 15th century

France or South Netherlands
L. 37 cm | Inv. no. W31

Horns were used to signal at the chase and in battle. This one was regarded as an important relic of St Hubert and was once richly decorated. It was reputedly being used by the saint while hunting, when he experienced a vision of a stag with a crucifix between its antlers. In 1468, the relic was given by the bishop of Liège to Charles the Bold, Duke of Burgundy. It had been preserved at Liège, where St Hubert had been bishop. A chapel dedicated to St Hubert was built to house the horn at Chauvirey-le-Châtel in France, where it remained for centuries until it was sold to Sir Richard Wallace.

SMOKING ROOM

MEDIEVAL AND EARLY MODERN WORKS OF ART

The Smoking Room exhibits mainly paintings and works of art from the medieval, Renaissance and Baroque periods, including many of the most prestigious pieces from Sir Richard Wallace's outstanding collection of Italian Renaissance maiolica.

The room, seen below in an early 20th-century photograph, had a sumptuous interior, with walls lined with Iznik-style tiles made by the Minton factory in Stoke-on-Trent and the floor laid with a patterned mosaic. A small section of this interior survives in the alcove at the north end of the room.

The Smoking Room, about 1912.

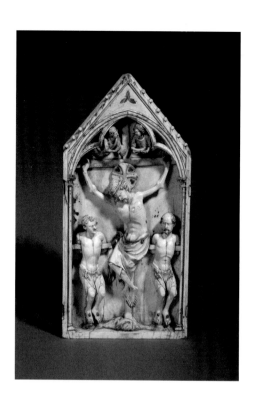

Christ Crucified between Two Thieves, about 1320

Paris, France
H. 26.6 cm | Inv. no. S247

In this sculpture, Christ is shown between two thieves: the good thief on Christ's right, who asked Christ to remember him, and the bad thief on Christ's left, who abused Christ. This ivory, which was once partly pigmented, is remarkable for the expressive naturalism and sculptural depth of the main figures. One of the greatest gothic ivories to survive, it was formerly the central section of a miniature altarpiece or the back of an altar, as evidenced by the remains of hinges on either side.

The Toilet of Bathsheba, about 1680-90

Francis van Bossuit (1635-1692)
H. 25 cm | Inv. no. S263

This ivory carving depicts a scene from the Old Testament in which King David, seen in the background on the roof of his palace, spied on and fell in love with Bathsheba, the wife of his general, Uriah. Van Bossuit has highlighted the erotic element of the story by showing Bathsheba having her hair braided by a maid after emerging from her bath, while an old woman sent by David presents her with a casket full of jewellery. The piece has always been regarded as an important work by Van Bossuit. It belonged to one of his major patrons, Petronella de la Court, a wealthy collector from Amsterdam.

Incense burners, mid-Qing Dynasty, probably Qianlong period (1736–95)

China
H. 167.6 cm | Inv. nos OA2367–8

These spectacular, pagoda-shaped incense burners are decorated with *cloisonné* enamel. This technique uses fine wires to delineate a design, and the resulting spaces are filled with enamel paste. Various auspicious motifs are represented on the burners, including dragons, cranes, peonies and the character for longevity (*shou*). Incense was used in domestic, scholarly, religious and palatial contexts in Imperial China. It was commonly formed into sticks that were placed in beds of sand and burnt in vessels. Incense smoke would then escape through the holes. The forms of incense burners often derived from ancient bronzes. The lower part of this pair is known as a *ding* – a traditional, three-legged ritual vessel.

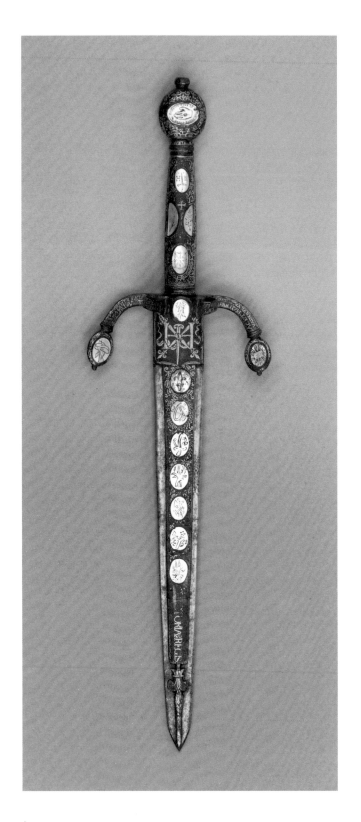

Dagger of Henri IV of France, 1599–1600

France
L. 36 cm | Inv. no. A790

Richly decorated in gold and set with a series of mother-of-pearl inlays, this superb dagger, together with a matching rapier, was presented to Henri IV of France by the city of Paris in 1600 on his marriage to Marie de' Medici; the linked initials of the king and his new queen appear on the hilt. Both main inscriptions glorify Henri IV with esoteric astrological references. It is not known when this dagger was separated from its rapier, now in the Musée de l'Armée, Paris. The separation probably occurred in the early 19th century, when the rapier became a treasured possession of Napoleon I, Emperor of the French, who carried it on campaign as a talisman. The dagger meanwhile found its way onto the Paris art market and was bought by Sir Richard Wallace in 1877.

Dish: *Women Bathing*, 1525

Workshop of Maestro Giorgio Andreoli
(about 1470–1555), central scene attributed
to Francesco Xanto Avelli (about 1486–about
1542) and border probably by Francesco Urbini
Dia. 44.6 cm | Inv. no. C66

Exquisitely painted, this monumental dish is an
outstanding example of the virtuosity achieved
by Andreoli's acclaimed maiolica workshop
in Gubbio, a small town in the Umbria region
of Italy. The inscription in lustre on the
back, dated 6 April 1525, proclaims proudly
that it was made in this workshop, which
was celebrated for the beauty of its lustre,
especially the distinctive ruby red. Gold and
ruby red lustre shine from the surface of this
beautiful dish. The bathing women are taken
from three Italian prints depicting mythological
subjects. The dish reflects the Renaissance
fascination with Classical Antiquity, as the
figures bathe in a pool with a marble front
that is inspired by ancient Roman precedents,
while the rim is flamboyantly decorated with
grotesques.

Dish, 1560–70

Iznik, Turkey
Dia. 47.4 cm | Inv. no. C199

This beautiful dish is wonderfully evocative
of the 16th-century Ottoman court culture in
which Iznik ceramics flourished. At its centre,
the glorious turquoise background, suggesting
perhaps a brilliant summer sky, is a perfect
foil for the fantastical, stylised peacock among
flowers and foliage. The delightful decoration
in the border, comprising split palmettes
interwoven with flowers and leaves, both
frames and extends the peacock's flower-
bedecked domain. The distinctive red, standing
out in relief, was a recent addition to the Iznik
palette, which became more vivid from about
mid-century. A key element in the popularity
of Iznik ceramics was the strong, clean white
ground. The inclusion of a bird at the centre of
an Iznik dish is very unusual at this early date.

Pendant, late 16th century

Germany
H. 5.2 cm | Inv. no. W89

One of the hallmarks of the Renaissance curiosity cabinet (*Kunstkammer*) was the juxtaposition of marvels from the natural world with showpieces of human ingenuity. This duality can be seen in the small sculptures or pieces of jewellery created from large misshapen 'baroque' pearls, which became especially popular at princely courts from the late 16th century. This particularly delightful pendant depicts a rabbit or hare, the flecked white enamel points suggesting the animal's fur.

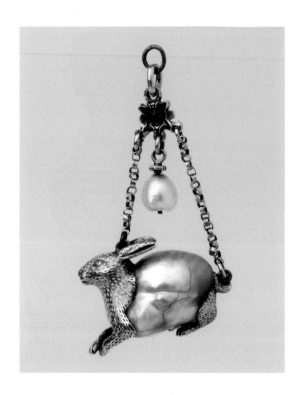

Ceremonial chain, late 15th century (chain) and 1499–1826 (shields)

Gorinchem, Netherlands
Dia. 50.8 cm | Inv. no. W32

This spectacular chain belonged to the Guild of St George in the Dutch town of Gorinchem. The small figure of the guild's patron slaying the dragon is incorporated in the foliage decoration. The guild was a voluntary civic guard, whose members were armed with crossbows. Dutch civic guards consisted of wealthy and influential citizens and owned impressive collections of ceremonial silver. The engraved shields commemorate the winners of an annual shooting competition, known as 'kings', who wore the chain on special occasions. The parrots within the chain refer to the fact that models of parrots or stuffed birds were traditionally used as targets for the competitions.

Wine cooler, 1574
Workshop of Flaminio Fontana (active 1571–91)
H. 40 cm | Inv. no. C107

Probably made for Cosimo I de' Medici, Grand Duke of Tuscany, this monumental wine cooler bears his device of a turtle with a mast on its back, illustrating his motto, *Festina lente* (Hasten slowly). The inscription on its base indicates that it was made in Fontana's maiolica workshop in Urbino in 1574; Cosimo died in April 1574. Wine coolers were kept on or below a buffet, filled with ice, snow or cold water, to keep wine cool during meals. The decoration of this exceptionally large cooler combines white-ground grotesques, vigorously sculpted monsters and a Roman naval battle scene derived, unusually, from a drawing. The water-based theme was appropriate to a wine cooler.

Basin, late 16th century–early 17th century
Follower of Bernard Palissy (about 1510–1590)
L. 49.3 cm | Inv. no. C174

Palissy, a Renaissance polymath and highly innovative self-taught potter, pioneered the production of lead-glazed earthenware incorporating life-cast reptiles, water creatures and plants. Palissy's interest in the imitation of nature through art was shared by many artists of the period. This basin is an excellent example of the type of rustic-style pottery for which Palissy is best known. He sold his first rustic basin to Henri II of France in 1556. This basin has been transformed into a pond or stream supporting an abundance of animal and plant life, including a snake, fish and crayfish. Perhaps it accompanied an ewer for hand washing during meals or simply served as a table ornament. Only a very small number of pieces are currently attributed firmly to Palissy himself.

ARMS AND ARMOUR GALLERY I

NON-EUROPEAN ARMS AND ARMOUR AND WORKS OF ART

Most of the arms and armour from beyond Western Europe now in the Collection were acquired by the 4th Marquess of Hertford in the 1860s, and Sir Richard Wallace continued to collect such material up to about 1880. This gallery includes outstanding works from the Ottoman Empire, Iran, India, China and Ghana. Many objects were newly made when purchased and reflect the taste for 'exotic' works of art in Paris and London at the time.

Wallace installed his collection of what was then known among collectors as 'Oriental' arms and armour on the east side of the first floor of Hertford House, as seen in the photograph below of about 1888. Trophies of arms formed large geometric patterns on the walls of the gallery, while the ceiling was decorated with gold stars on a deep blue background.

'Oriental' arms and armour displayed in today's East Gallery I, about 1888.

Rock crystal is a transparent, colourless quartz, which, although very hard, has from ancient times been carved into decorative and useful objects. This wine bowl is a rare surviving example of rock crystal produced for the Mughal court in the 17th century. The Mughals, the Muslim rulers of India, had a long and outstanding artistic tradition, particularly in architecture, textiles and metalwork, as well as carving in precious materials, such as jade and rock crystal. The decoration of this bowl is deliberately restrained in order to demonstrate the purity of the rock crystal.

Bowl, 17th century
North India
H. 7 cm | Inv. no. W111

Mosque lamp, about 1350–57
Cairo, Egypt
H. 39.4 cm | Inv. no. C512

This mosque lamp is one of some twenty that bear the blazon of the Great Amir Sayf al-Dīn Shaykhū al-'Umarī, a powerful Mamluk amir of the mid-14th century. Probably commissioned in his honour, the lamp depicts his blazon at the centre of six medallions. The red outlines and elaborate use of blue and gold are characteristic of mosque lamps from this period. If looked at closely, one can see a variety of imagery, including flowers and fish. When lit, its decoration would have inspired thoughts of a heavenly garden of paradise and symbolised God's presence. The thuluth inscription on the lamp is from the Qur'an and may be translated as: 'God is the light of the heavens and the earth; His light is like a niche in which there is a lamp'.

**Trophy head, 18th or
19th century**

Asante (Ghana)
H. 20 cm | Inv. no.
OA1683

This trophy head was made in the West
African state of Asante, in present-day Ghana.
The Asante people controlled extensive gold
resources and were renowned for the objects
they made from this precious metal. The head
is among the most important and famous works
of Asante art and depicts a defeated enemy
leader. The object would have been attached
to a ceremonial sword by the loop under its

chin. The head was among the treasures kept
in King Kofi Karikari's palace in Kumasi, which
was looted and destroyed by British forces
during the Third Anglo-Asante War (1873–4).
It was acquired by Garrard & Co. Ltd, the crown
jeweller in London. Sir Richard Wallace bought
it from them in 1874, along with a group of other
Asante objects, including swords and jewellery.

**Gold Cups of Eternal Stability 金甌永固杯,
1739–40 and 1740–41**

Beijing, China
H. 18.7 cm (W113) and H. 18 cm (W112) |
Inv. nos W113 and W112

These gold cups, decorated with kingfisher feathers, pearls and gemstones, were made for the Qianlong Emperor. As part of the New Year celebrations at the Forbidden City in Beijing, the emperor used the cup to drink *tusu* wine, a special herbal drink. This ceremony was intended to ensure the country's territorial integrity. The darker cup, made in the fourth year of Qianlong's reign, may have been the prototype, the model of which was adjusted, and two new cups were produced the following year; one is the second cup seen here. Sir Richard Wallace acquired the cups at an auction in Paris in 1872. The sale catalogue described them as coming from the Summer Palace, which had been looted and destroyed by French and British soldiers in 1860, during the Second Opium War (1856–60).

Helmet, late 18th century

India
Wt 1.3 kg | Inv. no. OA1769

The richly gold-overlaid helmet is of burnished steel, shaped to accommodate the topknot of hair that is worn by devout Sikhs; this type of helmet is therefore specifically Sikh in origin and one of only a handful to survive. Though it is a work of great craftsmanship, there is in fact a slight flaw in the metal of the helmet skull, just to one side, but it has been cleverly concealed by the craftsman, who has applied gold inlay in the shape of a bird directly over it. Another bird has been applied to the other side in order to balance the design.

Shield, 1848–9

Iran
Dia. 47.6 cm | Inv. no. OA1923

Although lacquered painting was a common art form in 19th-century Iran, it is usually found on pen boxes, mirror cases and other small objects; to find this type of painting on a shield is extremely unusual. Made when Iran was embroiled in turmoil and the Qajar monarchy was under existential threat from both tribal revolts in the east and an apocalyptic religious movement in the west, this shield is evidence that high-quality works of art continued to be commissioned even in turbulent times.

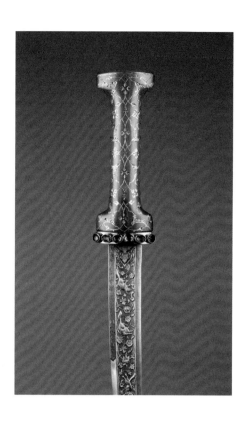

Dagger, last quarter of the 15th century
Iran or Central Asia
L. 34.4 cm | Inv. no. OA1414

The blade on this beautifully moulded and gold-inlaid dagger is a rare surviving example of a group of blades made in the Timurid Empire at the close of the 15th century. The decorative pattern on the blade is typical of the manuscript illumination of Herat. The dagger may have been made for Husayn Bayqara, the last Timurid sultan to wield effective political power, or one of his most important courtiers. It is possible that the craftsmen who made this dagger fled to the Safavid court in Tabriz following the capture of Herat by the Uzbek army in 1507, only to have been taken to Istanbul when the Ottomans occupied Tabriz seven years later.

Dagger, about 1620–40
North India
L. 39 cm | Inv. no. OA1415

Fashioned from a single piece of rock crystal, the hilt of this magnificent Mughal dagger is inlaid with gold and set with rubies, emeralds and diamonds. The name *Claud Martin* is lightly inscribed on one panel of the stone. Claude Martin was a Frenchman who fought against the British in India but changed sides following the siege and fall of Pondicherry in 1760–61. He joined the army of the British East India Company as an ensign, working his way up through the ranks to become major general in charge of the Lucknow Arsenal. He is recorded as having been an enthusiastic collector of princely arms and armour, and this dagger was once his.

Dagger, about 1615
North India
L. 35.1 cm | Inv. no. OA1409

The memoirs of the Mughal emperor Jahangir frequently mention the presentation of jewelled daggers as a way of bestowing imperial favour on important courtiers and princes. When Jahangir's son, Khurram, returned victorious from Central India in 1617, he was given the name 'Shah Jahan' and presented with many gifts, including a jewelled dagger. A portrait by Nadir al-Zaman, now in the Victoria and Albert Museum, London, is thought to depict this ceremony: it shows Shah Jahan in profile, with a peculiar dagger tucked into his belt. The *hamsa* bird (a mythical bird resembling a goose) decoration, as well as the knuckle-guard connecting to the gable, are both highly unusual features that help us identify the dagger in the painting with this dagger in the Collection.

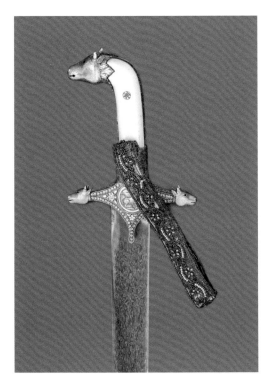

Sword, first quarter of the 19th century
North India
L. 91.6 cm | Inv. no. OA1404

This magnificent gold-mounted sword has traditionally been considered a personal sword of Maharaja Ranjit Singh, the 'Lion of the Punjab', based on its description in an 1865 exhibition catalogue. While it is a high-quality and finely decorated sword, there is no further evidence of this connection, and it may have been made at any of the north Indian courts. The scabbard fittings are consistent with an attribution to the court of Lucknow.

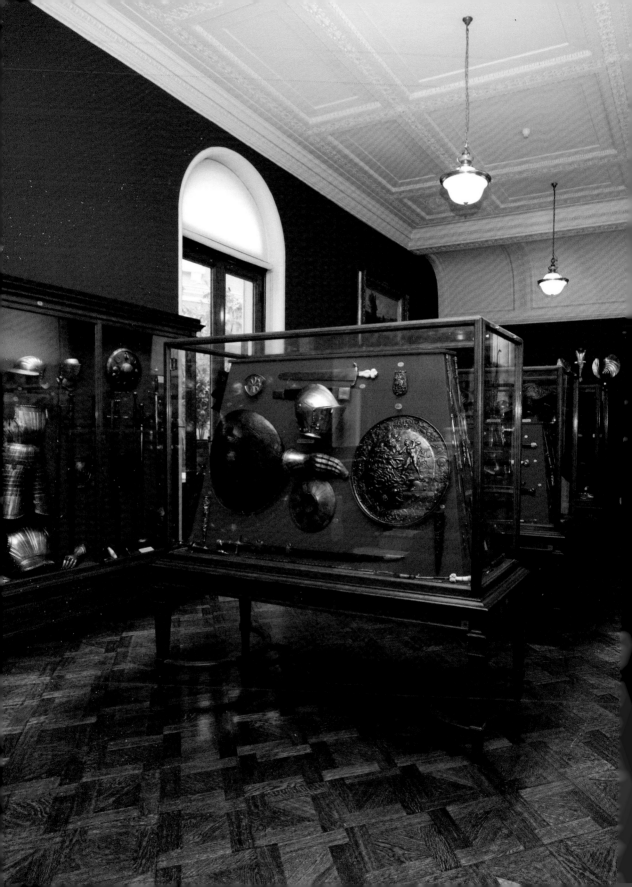

ARMS AND ARMOUR GALLERY II

EUROPEAN MEDIEVAL AND RENAISSANCE ARMS AND ARMOUR (10TH TO 16TH CENTURIES)

Sir Richard Wallace acquired most of his European weapons and armour in 1871–2, when he bought the collection of the comte de Nieuwerkerke, formerly superintendent of the arts under Napoleon III, Emperor of the French, as well as portions of the collection of Sir Samuel Rush Meyrick, a pioneering collector and early scholar of historical arms. This gallery displays some of the best-preserved medieval arms and armour in the world, alongside examples of the work of Renaissance master armourers, including Wolfgang Grosschedel of Landshut, creator of the finest armours of Philip II of Spain, and Konrad Seusenhofer of Innsbruck, court armourer to Maximilian I, Holy Roman Emperor.

During Sir Richard and Lady Wallace's lifetime, this gallery formed part of the stables, with the grooms' bedrooms on a mezzanine floor. Sir Richard's European arms and armour were originally displayed in one large room on the first floor, today's West Gallery III, directly above this gallery.

European arms and armour displayed in today's West Gallery III, about 1888.

Field armour, about 1505

South Germany, probably Nuremburg
Wt 19.6 kg | Inv. no. A22

This field armour is an exceptionally important example of the art of the early 16th-century armourer. It is decorated with etched vines running along the edges of the breast- and backplates and the crowned cipher of Wladislas II of Bohemia and Hungary in the centre of the chest, indicating the allegiance of the owner. Below the crowned *W* is an etched scroll bearing an enigmatic acronym. Based on this, it is possible that the letters stand for an expression, such as *Gott Ist Gewisslich Mein Erloeser* ('God is surely my Redeemer'). Religious statements are often found on armour, added in the belief that the harness could provide spiritual as well as physical protection.

Visored bascinet, about 1390–1410

Probably France
Wt 2 kg (without visor) | Inv. no. A69

Helmets of this form were used throughout Europe in the late 14th and early 15th centuries and became icons of the Hundred Years' War. The distinctive muzzle provided an excellent glancing surface, with its pointed shape making it difficult for incoming weapons to gain purchase. The visor can be easily removed by pulling out the pins holding it in place. With the visor removed, the wearer could see and breath more easily. The visor might be worn early in a battle, when the wearer was more likely to be hit by fast-moving threats like arrows and javelins, but for hand-to-hand combat, vision and ventilation became more important and the open-faced configuration preferable.

Close-helmet, about 1530
Nuremburg, Germany
Wt 3.4 kg | Inv. no. A158

This fabulously sculpted close-helmet exemplifies the best work of the great armour-making city of Nuremberg. The visor of this very fine piece has been embossed in the German 'grotesque' or 'vernacular' style, which usually incorporates human or animal masks. Such visors were worn on a variety of ceremonial and festive occasions. Like other surviving animal mask visors made in south Germany about the same time, this piece represents its subject, in this case an eagle's head, through an impressive demonstration of steel embossing. The sculpted head is further embellished with delicately etched detailing and two original copper-alloy rivets forming the eagle's eyes.

Armour for the German Joust of Peace, about 1500–20

Nuremburg and Augsburg, Germany
Wt 40.9 kg | Inv. no. A23

Unlike field armour, a jousting harness was often very heavy. This example is nearly twice the weight of German war equipment of the same period. This is because it was designed for peaceful sporting contests, not warfare. This armour was designed for a type of joust called the *Deutsches Gestech*, or 'German Joust of Peace', a form often held to celebrate social occasions, such as an aristocratic wedding or diplomatic visit. The style was popular because it was relatively safe but still extremely impressive. The heavy armour was constructed to withstand hugely powerful impacts, delivered with very thick, long lances. Sometimes the collisions were so violent that the riders and their horses were knocked to the ground together.

Falchion, 1546–69

Italy
L. 77 cm | Inv. no. A710

This extremely fine falchion was made for Cosimo I de' Medici, Duke of Florence, later Grand Duke of Tuscany, one of the most powerful Italian princes of the 16th century, whose coat of arms is etched on the blade. During the 16th century, it became fashionable for powerful aristocrats to associate themselves with the heroes of the ancient world. Greek and Roman culture had been brought back to life in the architecture, literature, art and military display of the Renaissance. Artists and writers of the time imagined the ancient world as a 'heroic age' inhabited by superhuman warriors, such as Achilles, Hector and Hercules. Like the fantastical embossed armour of this period, this sword expresses the Renaissance prince's desire to emulate these heroes.

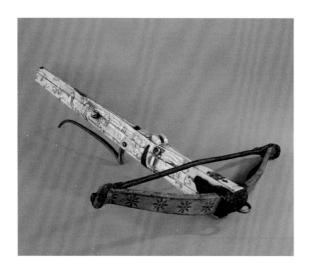

Hunting crossbow, 1487–1500

Bavaria, Germany
L. 72 cm | Inv. no. A1032

Sumptuously decorated, this is one of the finest surviving examples of a late medieval crossbow. Its stock is veneered with white antler depicting various subjects, including courtly love, the hunt, St George and the Dragon, and Adam and Eve. In addition to its superlative craftsmanship, this weapon also represents the cutting edge of mid-15th-century technology. The bow is made of tempered steel, rather than the more typical composite horn and sinew, giving it superior range and power. Although it is just as powerful as contemporary war crossbows, if not more so, the rich decoration on this example suggests that it was a prestigious piece used for hunting. An essential part of medieval life, hunting was a favoured sport among the aristocracy.

Mask visor, 1529

Hans Seusenhofer (1470–1555), etched by Leonard Meurl (died 1547) | Inv. no. A204

Once part of a large garniture, this visor may have been designed for parade use, although mask visors were worn in combat as well, especially in a form of mock combat called the 'Hungarian' or 'hussar' tournament. This was a military game fought in teams, in which one side appeared as European knights, while their opponents appeared as Ottoman warriors. In this way, the hussar tournament represented the conflict between Christians and Muslims. This visor has been embossed and chased with a prominent nose and long moustache, ethnic features, which, at the time, were associated with Hungarians.

Saddle, 1440–60

Germany
Wt 3 kg | Inv. no. A408

This extremely rare late medieval saddle is comprised of a wooden frame or 'tree', which has been skilfully overlaid with panels of carved antler and enriched with infills of hard, coloured wax. The decoration includes a conversation between courtly lovers, in which the lady asks, 'And if the war should end?', to which her lover responds, 'I will rejoice ever to be thine'. Such richly decorated saddles were used by aristocrats for hunting, parades and on other formal occasions. Despite their total lack of padding or upholstery, they are very comfortable to sit in because of their graceful shape, designed to provide a perfect fit with the anatomy of the rider.

ARMS AND ARMOUR GALLERY III

EUROPEAN RENAISSANCE ARMS AND ARMOUR (15TH TO 17TH CENTURIES)

The Collection contains some of the most spectacular Renaissance arms and armour preserved in the United Kingdom. Kings, knights and aristocrats commissioned beautifully decorated weapons and armour for war, jousts, tournaments, hunting and parade. Some of the finest examples of the armourer's art are displayed in this gallery, including masterpieces by Jacob Halder, master of the royal armour workshop of Elizabeth I of England, and Kolman Helmschmid, court armourer to Charles V, Holy Roman Emperor.

The space was formerly part of Sir Richard and Lady Wallace's stables and was converted into a museum gallery between 1897 and 1900.

European arms and armour displayed in today's West Gallery III, about 1888.

Garniture for the field, 1587–8

Jacob Halder (died 1608)

Wt 36.7 kg (with plackart) | Inv. no. A62

Henry VIII of England founded his Greenwich armour workshop in 1515, primarily to make fighting equipment for his own personal use. However, by the reign of Elizabeth I of England, the workshop was devoted entirely to making armours for the queen's close supporters, who bought special licences granting them this privilege. One such licensee was the diplomat and writer Sir Thomas Sackville, Lord Buckhurst, who served as a cavalry commander in the defence against invasion by the Spanish Armada in 1588. It is possible that this armour was made for him to wear in this role. The garniture is richly decorated with etched and gilt strapwork and borders. Its design also reflects contemporary fashions, such as the pigeon-breasted form (called 'peascod') seen in men's doublets of the late 16th century.

Close-helmet for the tournament, about 1555

Attributed to Conrad Richter (1520–1570)

Wt 5.6 kg | Inv. no. A188

In 1555, in preparation for a tournament in Vienna, Ferdinand I, Holy Roman Emperor, commissioned a series of matching golden garnitures for himself and his three sons: the future Maximilian II, Archduke Ferdinand II of Tyrol and Archduke Charles II of Styria. All four of these rich tournament armours had matching etched and gilt decoration. This helmet is all that remains of the emperor's armour and has clearly seen fierce combat. The crest and visor are battered with sword-cuts. Indeed, the left side of the brow had become so scarred during the armour's working lifetime that at some point an additional reinforcing plate was added. This plate has been skilfully etched and gilt to match but is clearly by a different artist.

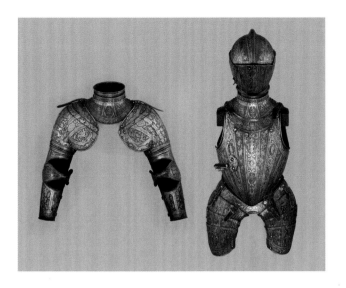

The garniture to which these pieces, gilt and etched with scrolling foliage and classical figures, belong was made for Wolf Dietrich von Raitenau, Prince-Bishop of Salzburg. The identity of the maker is uncertain, although it might have been created in the workshop of Della Cesa, foremost of the late 16th-century Italian armourers and master of a large operation in Milan. It provided pieces for all primary war and sporting roles, including complete armours for the field, joust, free tourney and foot combat at the barriers. The elements in the Collection comprise the cuirass (body armour) and close-helmet for the joust and the arm and shoulder defences for foot combat at the barriers. They would never have all been worn together.

Parts of a garniture for the field, joust and tournament, 1587

Milan, Italy, possibly by Pompeo della Cesa (1536/8–1610)
Wt 17.6 kg | Inv. no. A60

Tournament gauntlet, 1550

Matthäus Frauenpreiss I (1505–1549),
etched by Jörg Sorg II (1517–1603)
Wt 0.6 kg | Inv. no. A270

The decoration on this fine gauntlet for the free tourney, a type of formal combat fought between teams of armoured knights, identifies it as belonging to a very large garniture made for the future Maximilian II, Holy Roman Emperor, between 1549 and 1550. One of the greatest German garnitures, this huge 'king's garniture' provided all required protective equipment for war, as well as tournament combat on horseback and on foot and several forms of joust. The decoration is not especially complicated, composed of wide etched and gilt strapwork bands framed by much narrower strips of etched cabling. However, the quality, of both the plates themselves and their ornamentation, is exemplary.

Parts of a field armour, 1525–30

Kolman Helmschmid (1471–1532), etched by Daniel Hopfer (1470–1536)
Wt 16.3 kg | Inv. no. A30

Although it is not marked, this outstanding armour is clearly the work of Helmschmid, one of the greatest armourers who ever lived. The Helmschmids were a dynasty of armourers based in Augsburg since the Middle Ages, famous for their unrivalled skill and inventiveness. This armour may have been commissioned by Charles V, Holy Roman Emperor, as a gift for a relative, perhaps his younger brother, the future Ferdinand I. It displays embossed, etched and gilt decoration of the most exceptional quality. The etched decoration can be firmly attributed to Hopfer, one of the first artists to apply etching as a process in printmaking. Before this innovation, etching had been almost exclusively employed as a technique for the decoration of armour.

Equestrian armour, 1532 and 1536

Hans Ringler
Wt 26.4 kg (man's armour) and 28.5 kg (horse's armour) | Inv. no. A29

Otto Heinrich, or 'Ottheinrich', was a powerful German prince, soldier, patron of the arts and, later in his career, champion of the Protestant Reformation. Ottheinrich had many fine armours. They were worn on military campaigns for personal protection and as the status symbols associated with a ruler of great prestige. The colour of this armour reflected the tinctures of Ottheinrich's coat of arms – black, gold and silver. The armour as we see it today is a composite, made up of parts from several of Ottheinrich's armours. This is revealed by the decorative motifs within the gilt bands. The pauldrons (shoulder plates) and cuirass (body armour) share the same pattern, featuring birds and small children. Other parts have a different design of scrolling, flowering foliage.

Equestrian armour, 1480 (with later restorations)

Possibly by Ulrich Rämbs
Wt 27.2 kg (man's armour) and 30.1 kg (horse's armour) | Inv. no. A21

This complete war armour for man and horse is a world-famous image of the medieval European knight. The horse armour is by far the most important part of the ensemble. Only three of these survive in the world today, and this is the only one preserved complete as originally made. The rider's armour is a composite, made up in the 19th century using some original pieces, combined with restored and replicated elements to complete the figure. Until the 19th century, the armour was preserved in the ancestral home of the Freyberg family at Schloss Hohenaschau in Bavaria. About 1850, its contents were sold, acquired by the comte de Nieuwerkerke in 1867 and then sold to Sir Richard Wallace, along with the rest of the Nieuwerkerke collection, in 1871.

Parts of a parade armour, 1575–90

Lucio Marliani, called Piccinino (1538–1607)
Wt 10.9 kg | Inv. no. A51

The decoration on this parade armour beautifully expresses the classically inspired approach that defines the High Mannerist period, in which detailed, life-like figures and scenes are placed within strange, improbable landscapes made up of architectural, animal and plant elements. It features mythological and allegorical figures contained within strapwork bands filled with cartouches and arabesques overlaid in silver and surrounded with gold foliate scrolls. The original owner of this armour is unknown, although there is an old and plausible tradition that it was made for Alfonso II d'Este, Duke of Ferrara, Modena, Reggio and Chartres, a great patron of literature and the arts in late 16th-century Italy.

ARMS AND ARMOUR GALLERY IV

LATER EUROPEAN ARMS AND ARMOUR
(16TH TO 19TH CENTURIES)

The array of sporting guns, rifles and pistols in this gallery includes a large number of extravagantly decorated 16th- and early 17th-century wheel-lock firearms, together with an impressive group of magnificent civilian flint-lock guns of the Napoleonic period. Several of the weapons here were made for European rulers, including Louis XIII and Louis XIV of France and Nicholas I of Russia. It is one of the finest collections of early firearms in the United Kingdom.

The space was formerly part of Sir Richard and Lady Wallace's coach house and stable yard and was converted into a museum gallery between 1897 and 1900.

European arms and armour displayed in today's West Gallery III, about 1888.

Although capable of being fired, this small cannon, with its lavish decoration, was clearly only ever intended for ceremonial use. It is signed by Mazzaroli, a member of one of the three families of bronze founders who supplied the Venetian Republic with much of its artillery from the 15th century through to its fall in 1797. The main decorative scene on the upper surface of the barrel depicts Jupiter, seated on an eagle, hurling thunderbolts at a group of Titans, who struggle and cower beneath an avalanche of rocks. Around the muzzle is a frieze of the Rape of the Sabines. The sculptural quality of the decoration is even more evident on the cannon's base, with a scene of Hercules struggling with two men.

Cannon, 1688

Giovanni Mazzaroli (1668–1744)
L. 141 cm (cannon barrel) | Inv. no. A1245

Parade shield of Henri II of France, 1558–9

North Italy, probably Milan
H. 67.3 cm | Inv. no. A325

This parade shield was probably made in Milan, where armourers were masters of embossing and chasing relief decoration in steel. Here, these techniques have been used to create a complex pseudo-historical scene, decorated with silver and gold, on its surface. It represents an episode from the Punic Wars (264–146 BCE), fought between the Romans and the Carthaginians. The scene seems to be an elaborate commemoration of the surrender of English-held Calais to the French in 1558, which was considered a symbolic victory to Henri II of France. The connection with the king is emphasised by the interlaced crescents and *D* device of his mistress, Diane de Poitiers, at the top of the shield. The *D*s also form the king's double *H* cipher.

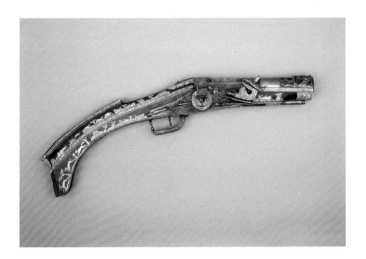

Wheel-lock firework launcher, 1590
Germany
L. 65.4 cm | Inv. no. A1077

This rare and fascinating gun was formerly thought to be some form of grenade launcher or to have been made for the discharge of heavy loads of shot. However, its barrel width is too small and the decoration too rich for such functions. Instead, it is more likely to have been intended to launch fireworks. By the end of the 16th century, firework displays had become an almost standard part of courtly festivals. Elizabeth I of England regarded these displays as so vital to the enhancement and reflection of the luxury and glory of her court that she created an entirely new post of 'master of fire' to devise them.

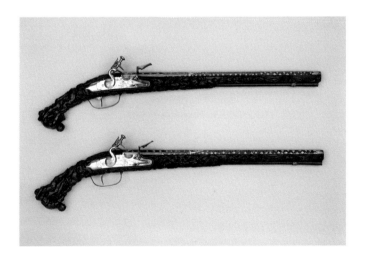

Pair of flint-lock pistols of Louis XIV of France, 1659–60
France
L. 59.7 cm | Inv. nos A1209–10

Made for Louis XIV of France, this extraordinary pair of pistols are of the very highest quality, the fine, faceted barrels heat blued and overlaid in gold, their whole lengths covered with the royal fleur-de-lys. The dark walnut stocks are entirely carved in high relief with depictions of Hercules fighting the Nemean Lion and Samson slaughtering the Philistines. The Herculean theme is continued elsewhere in the decoration through lions' skins, lion masks and clubs. The combat is also depicted on the barrels. Each pistol bears an inscription presenting Hercules as a personification of France, while the combat with the lion is a metaphor referring to a French military campaign.

Presentation hunting knife, 1860

Paris, France
L. 69.7 cm | Inv. no. A707

The latest edged weapon in the Collection is also the only one directly associated with the 4th Marquess of Hertford. This strange yet beautifully made hunting knife, with a hilt in the form of a Native American fighting two mountain lions, was given to him about 1860 by Napoleon III, Emperor of the French. The scabbard is engraved on the back with the French imperial device encircled by the collar of the Legion of Honour, of which both men were members. The blade appears to be a relic associated with Napoleon I, one of many 'watered' crucible steel blades made in the Caucasus but thought at the time to have been brought back to France after the Egyptian campaign of 1798–1801.

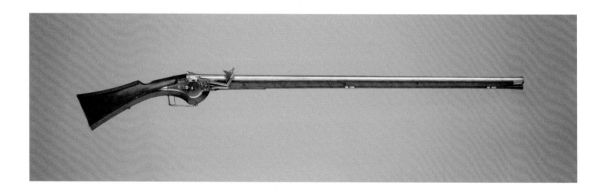

Wheel-lock gun with ramrod, about 1620

France
L. 132 cm | Inv. no. A1111

Louis XIII of France had a strong interest in hunting and had a passion for sporting guns. He patronised several master gunmakers and collected hundreds of guns, from plain, functional pieces to exquisitely decorated wheel-lock and flint-lock firearms. This is one of two of the king's personal guns now in the Collection. It is relatively plain in terms of decoration yet is supremely elegant in form. Stocked in French walnut and mounted in plain steel, it represents a radical departure from the heavily ornate weapons popular in the previous century.

Rapier, about 1585–1620

Italy (hilt) and probably Toledo, Spain (blade)

L. 119.2 cm | Inv. no. A609

One of the finest rapiers in the Collection, this piece is composed of a fine blade, apparently Spanish, mounted into an Italian swept-hilt decorated with an ingenious combination of gilding and gold overlay. The surfaces of the hilt bars have been divided into small heart-shaped, interlocking panels, decorated using two schemes that contrast alternately, somewhat like a chessboard. One form of decoration involves chiselled and fire-gilt designs in relief, while the other, forming the negative space between, takes the form of very fine foliate scrolls, overlaid in gold against a blackened ground.

Cased long gun of Nicholas I of Russia, 1805

Nicolas-Noël Boutet
(1761–1833)

L. 102 cm | Inv. no. A1126

This magnificent hunting piece was probably commissioned by Napoleon I, Emperor of the French. It was made by Boutet, artist-director of the Versailles Arms Manufactory. The cased set, which also includes all the instruments needed to clean, load and fire the weapon, was later owned by Nicholas I of Russia, his cipher appearing on the case lid. The two barrels are positioned one on top of the other, each being fired by its own half lock. One barrel is smooth bore, designed for hunting small game, while the other is rifled, designed for shooting large game. The barrels are richly decorated, being heat blued and inlaid with small gold stars, and the muzzle is engraved with thunderclouds and lightning bolts.

FOUNDERS' COURT

The Founders' Court contains marble busts of the three principal founders of the Collection: Richard Seymour-Conway, 4th Marquess of Hertford; his likely son, Sir Richard Wallace; and Lady Wallace, who bequeathed the works of art on the ground and first floors of Hertford House to the British nation.

Richard Seymour-Conway,
4th Marquess of Hertford,
about 1872

Charles-Auguste Lebourg
(1829–1906)
H. 66 cm | Inv. no. S44

Richard Seymour-Conway, 4th Marquess of Hertford, was one of the most important art collectors of his age, and he had a pivotal role in shaping the character of the Collection. He lived the greater part of his life in Paris and had a passion for 18th-century French painting and decorative arts. He also collected 17th-century Dutch and Flemish masters, 19th-century French paintings and non-European arms and armour. Hertford never married. It is likely that Sir Richard Wallace was his illegitimate son.

Sir Richard Wallace, 1899

Emmanuel Hannaux (1855–1934)
H. 66 cm | Inv. no. S46

Sir Richard Wallace was born in London but spent most of his life in Paris. As secretary to the 4th Marquess of Hertford, Wallace often acquired art on his behalf, becoming a connoisseur in his own right. In 1870, he inherited the greater part of Hertford's renowned art collection. He then moved to London, settled at Hertford House and expanded the collection, acquiring mainly medieval and Renaissance works of art and European arms and armour. Wallace was a distinguished philanthropist and a generous lender to exhibitions. Queen Victoria granted him a baronetcy in 1871 for his philanthropy during the Siege of Paris.

Lady Wallace, about 1872

Charles-Auguste Lebourg (1829–1906)
H. 71 cm | Inv. no. S45

Julie Amélie Charlotte Castelnau, later Lady Wallace, was born in Paris. She and Richard Wallace married in 1871, after over thirty years together. While little is known about her personal interest in art, she certainly shared Wallace's commitment to philanthropy. In England, she experienced social animosity, largely due to her humble origins, reluctance to speak English, shyness, and the fact that she and Wallace had an illegitimate son, born in 1840. Yet, after her husband's death, it was she who bequeathed the celebrated art collection kept at Hertford House to the British nation in 1897.

LANDING

THE FRANÇOIS BOUCHER ROOM

The Landing serves as the main orientation point on the first floor. It is hung with an outstanding ensemble of paintings by François Boucher, first painter to Louis XV of France, favoured artist of Madame de Pompadour and arguably the single most influential artist of the 18th century. With stunning examples of his mythological and allegorical compositions, his pastorals, a domestic scene and his late portrait of Pompadour herself, the Landing showcases nearly every genre of painting in which this remarkably prolific and versatile artist worked.

Hertford House was built between 1777 and 1782 for the 4th Duke of Manchester. After his death in 1788, it was occupied for several years by the Spanish ambassador. In 1797, the 2nd Marquess of Hertford took up residence. His alterations included the addition of a first floor to the original low wings and the erection of a veranda over the entrance portico.

The Landing, about 1888.

The Rising of the Sun and *The Setting of the Sun*, **1752**

François Boucher (1703–1770)
H. 318 x W. 261 cm | Inv. nos P485–6

These paintings were commissioned by Madame de Pompadour, the mistress to Louis XV of France. They served as models for tapestries for the king's bedroom at the Château de Bellevue, Pompadour's country retreat. The paintings themselves were installed on the ground floor of the same house. They show the nymph Tethys assisting the classical deity Apollo as he sets out to drive the chariot of the sun across the sky, then welcoming him back after a day's work. This iconography celebrated Pompadour's influential role in French politics because the reference to Apollo, god of the sun, clearly designated Louis XV, whose predecessor, Louis XIV, had been known as the 'Sun King'.

Cupid and Psyche, about 1730

Filippo della Valle (1698–1768)
H. 84.4 cm | Inv. no. S22

This sculpture depicts Cupid, god of love, and the beautiful mortal woman Psyche. The group is by Della Valle, who enjoyed a successful career in Rome but was somewhat forgotten after his death. His elegant style has much in common with that of French 18th-century sculptors. The group was historically attributed to French sculptor Claude-Augustin Cayot, mainly on the basis of a false signature inscribed on the base. However, research has revealed that the group is a documented work by Della Valle. Cayot's signature was applied later, probably by a dealer. They may have had the 4th Marquess of Hertford in mind as a buyer, as he already owned a sculpture by Cayot.

Madame de Pompadour, 1759

François Boucher (1703–1770)
H. 91 x W. 68 cm | Inv. no. P418

After her relationship with Louis XV of France became platonic in about 1750, Madame de Pompadour commissioned a series of works of art with friendship and fidelity as their central theme. This portrait, probably the last Boucher painted of his patron, evokes these ideals through its inclusion of a sculpture depicting Friendship consoling Love, which was based on the work of the 18th-century sculptor Jean-Baptiste Pigalle. The presence of Pompadour's pet spaniel, Inès, shown seated on the bench beside her mistress, also makes reference to the emotions of comfort and security that come with lasting friendship.

SMALL DRAWING ROOM

THE EARLY 18TH CENTURY

This room illustrates stylistic changes during the French Regency (1715–23) and the early reign of Louis XV of France, which saw a relaxation of the tight control Louis XIV held over the French court and the development of a freer, more decorative style called the Rococo. Antoine Watteau introduced the *fête galante* to Paris, which was a form of painting showing idealised scenes of elegant people in the countryside. This subject, as well as his brilliant painterly style, referring to Peter Paul Rubens and the Venetians, became immediately successful with contemporary collectors. Theatre and music were major features of this new world. At the same time, East Asian objects and techniques, such as lacquer and porcelain, became highly popular.

In Sir Richard and Lady Wallace's day, this room was known as the Reynolds Drawing Room. In it hung most of the superb group of paintings by Joshua Reynolds in the Collection.

The Small Drawing Room, about 1888.

Les Champs Elisées, 1720–21

Antoine Watteau (1684–1721)

H. 31.2 x W. 41 cm | Inv. no. P389

Les Champs Elisées evokes the dream of ideal country life as imagined by a wealthy urban elite. The relationships between the young fashionable people are unclear. The standing man on the right is contemplating the women in front of him, while the sculpture of a nude woman above his head suggests the licentious nature of his thoughts. Behind the elegantly dressed crowd in the foreground, another group performs a country dance. This painting, which depicts beautifully dressed aristocrats disporting themselves in an ideal parkland environment, perfectly embodies the genre of the *fête galante* that is so closely associated with Watteau.

One of Lancret's most original creations, this painting marks a new departure in his art as well as in portraiture and the depiction of dance. Marie-Anne de Cupis de Camargo was one of the first great virtuoso ballerinas of the Paris Opera. Lancret convinces the viewer of the theatrical veracity of the image through the observation of details such as the dress and ballet position *à demi-pointe*. The scene unfolds in a park landscape. More than a theatrical backdrop, this setting lends the subject a poetic quality and creates the ideal framework for the dancer's artistic persona.

***Mademoiselle de Camargo Dancing,* 1730**

Nicolas Lancret (1690–1743)

H. 41.7 x W. 54.5 cm | Inv. no. P393

Chest-of-drawers, 1735–40

Antoine-Robert Gaudreaus
(1682–1746)

H. 93.3 cm | Inv. no. F85

This is one of the most excitingly rococo pieces of furniture in the Collection. Its double-bowed outline and elaborate gilt-bronze mounts, including palm ornament, dragons and volute feet, suggest a date of between 1735 and 1740, when the fashion for designs such as this was at its height. The female gilt-bronze mask in the centre is probably influenced by similarly costumed heads in engravings after Antoine Watteau.

Cartel clock, about 1747

Attributed to Charles Cressent
(1685–1768)
H. 135.9 cm | Inv. no. F92

The cabinetmaker Cressent was
frequently fined by the guild
authorities on suspicion of casting
furnishing bronzes (such as clock
cases and fire-dogs), thereby
transgressing his authorisation
as a cabinetmaker. This clock
was probably among works
sold in 1749 to pay off his debts.
The superb gilt-bronze case,
with figures of Love triumphing
over Time, is certainly closer
to sculpture than furniture, to
which Cressent has made a small
concession with the oak carcase
and Boulle marquetry on the sides.

Voulez-vous triompher des Belles?, 1714–17

Antoine Watteau (1684–1721)

H. 35.9 x W. 27 cm | Inv. no. P387

A masterful example of Watteau's poetic meditations on manners, courtship and love conveyed through delicate draughtsmanship and exquisite, shimmering brushstrokes. Harlequin's awkward, lunging gesture towards Columbine demonstrates his inability to restrain his physical desire beneath the requisite social grace. This is contrasted with the calm of the group in the background, where two lovers sit bathed in light and listening to a guitarist, in harmony with the music and each other, their mutual feeling symbolised by the roses in their hair and those shown growing beside them. The presence of two other *commedia dell'arte* characters, Crispin and Pierrot, behind the lovers reinforces the mood of theatrical ambiguity.

Pair of ewers,
1725–35 (Chinese porcelain) and
1745–9 (French mounts)

China, gilt-bronze mounts made in France
H. 29.8 cm | Inv. nos F105–6

Luxury goods dealers in 18th-century Paris often imported Chinese porcelain, which they then had fitted with extravagant gilt-bronze mounts. These precious goods represented the height of fashion and complemented the taste for Asian lacquer furniture at this time. The mounts on these pieces have been struck with the crowned C mark, which means that they were sold in France sometime between 1745 and 1749. The style of the mounts, cast and chased with naturalistically detailed flowers, buds, bulrushes, shells and weeds, is entirely consistent with the date suggested by their marks.

F105

LARGE DRAWING ROOM

BOULLE FURNITURE AND NETHERLANDISH PAINTINGS

In Sir Richard and Lady Wallace's lifetime, the Large Drawing Room was then, as now, dominated by monumental Boulle furniture, including the enormous bookcase known as the Londonderry Cabinet, and large Netherlandish paintings. In 18th-century France, this particular juxtaposition was much admired by collectors and was often augmented, as here, with bronzes and porcelain.

In the early 19th century, this room and the adjoining Oval Drawing Room were used for entertaining. The 2nd Marchioness of Hertford was famous for the events she hosted at Hertford House, such as the splendid ball she held in 1814 to celebrate the defeat and exile of Napoleon I, Emperor of the French, to the island of Elba.

The Large Drawing Room, about 1888.

A Family Group in a Landscape, **1647**

Gonzales Coques (1614–1684)

H. 113 x W. 171 cm | Inv. no. P92

One of the finest of Coques's portraits, *A Family Group in a Landscape* depicts a sophisticated ensemble of figures. The father of the family decorously holds his wife's hand while indicating the return of his sons from the hunt, which until shortly before the date of this painting had been an exclusive privilege of the aristocracy. A sister carrying a basket of fruit, perhaps indicating her hopes for a fruitful marriage, accompanies the boys. The background appears to be by another hand.

The Londonderry Cabinet, about 1775

Étienne Levasseur (1721–1798)

H. 182 cm | Inv. no. F390

Formed from seven different elements, this magnificent bookcase has three large cupboards fitted with pinewood shelves and closed by glazed double doors, and four flanking pilasters veneered with Boulle marquetry. The gilt-bronze mounts on the front and sides include bearded male masks, winged infants and mythological groups of Apollo and Marsyas and Apollo and Daphne. It is a reinterpretation of a design by André-Charles Boulle made by Levasseur at a time when art collectors highly valued Boulle's work from earlier in the 18th century.

**Still Life with a Monkey, about
1670–95**

Attributed to Jan Jansz. de Heem
(1650–in or after 1695)
H. 118 x W. 169.5 cm | Inv. no. P76

This ambitious composition is one of the finest works
attributed to De Heem. The inclusion of a live monkey
with still-life elements imitates earlier Flemish still-life
painters, such as Frans Snyders and Joannes Fyt. The
profusion of fruit, vegetables, crustacea, glass, silver and
porcelain afford the artist the opportunity to display his
considerable imitative skill. On a deeper level, the subject
may be seen as a celebration of the fruits of civilisation,
trade, peace and prosperity with the inclusion of imported
objects, such as the Chinese porcelain bowls. In contrast,
the viewer is reminded of the transitory nature of human
life and the dangers of overindulgence in material excess
by the inclusion of the broken column and classical frieze.

Wardrobe, about 1700

Attributed to André-Charles
Boulle (1642–1732)

H. 255 cm | Inv. no. F61

This grand wardrobe is one of two of the same model in the
Collection. The main purpose of the piece was for display, but
it was also fitted with shelves for storage. The figurative gilt-
bronze mounts on the doors represent Apollo and Daphne on
one side and Apollo flaying Marsyas on the other, mythological
stories derived from Ovid's *Metamorphoses*. The wardrobe was
once in the collection of the dukes of Buckingham at Stowe
House. The interior was lined with peach-blossom silk and
fitted with gilt-bronze brackets and hooks to hold the clothes
of Queen Victoria when she visited Stowe in 1845, three years
before the 4th Marquess of Hertford bought the wardrobe.

S167

Pair of vases: *The Triumph of Thetis*, probably 18th century

After François Girardon (1628–1715)
H. 44.4 cm | Inv. nos S167–8

These vases depict scenes from the Triumph of Thetis, a sea nymph who was the mother of Achilles. She is shown accompanied by her followers, fellow sea nymphs (Nereids), Tritons, marine centaurs, a marine goat (capricorn), dolphins and little children. The vases have similarities in composition to two much larger marble vases completed by Girardon in 1683 for the gardens at the Palace of Versailles. Probably cast after the sculptor's death, they may well preserve the compositions of Girardon's original wax models for the marble vases and are notable for the freshness and vivacity of the handling, which contrasts with the heavy formality of much French sculpture of this period.

Mantel clock, about 1768

Movement by Ferdinand Berthoud (1727–1807)
H. 47.5 cm | Inv. no. F267

Designed by the young sculptor Laurent Guiard, this model of clock was first made for Madame Geoffrin, a society hostess famed for holding artistic and literary soirées. According to her will, she kept the clock in her bedroom. She admired it so much that she commissioned another version to be made for the celebrated Enlightenment literary figure Denis Diderot. It became a popular model. The reading figure symbolises the good use of time but may also be a portrait of Madame Geoffrin. The plinth was made by the cabinetmaker Joseph Baumhauer.

OVAL DRAWING ROOM

FRENCH ROYAL AND ARISTOCRATIC TASTE

Known as the Octagon Room, this room was used by the 2nd Marchioness of Hertford as an entertaining space and ballroom. The chimney-piece, dating to about 1785, is the only original one to survive in situ at Hertford House. Sir Richard Wallace displayed his impressive collection of miniatures here.

The Oval Drawing Room, about 1888.

The Avignon Clock, 1771

Gilt-bronze case by Pierre Gouthière (1732–1813)
H. 68.5 cm | Inv. no. F258

A stunning example of the skills of the Parisian bronzeworker Gouthière, and considered to be one of his masterpieces, this clock is an example of the way in which clock cases were increasingly treated as pieces of figurative sculpture in the second half of the 18th century. The sculptor Louis-Simon Boizot was commissioned to make the terracotta model for the clock, from which the gilt-bronze model was made. The clock was presented by the grateful city of Avignon to the marquis de Rochechouart, a senior military figure who had been commanded by Louis XV of France to take Avignon back from papal control. The figures depicted on the clock are river gods representing the Rhône and the Durance, two rivers running through Avignon, and the city's coat of arms appears on the upright shield.

Fall-front desk, about 1776

Martin Carlin (1730–1785), porcelain plaques from the Sèvres Manufactory
H. 118.6 cm | Inv. no. F304

Sèvres porcelain plaques were first made for use on furniture in the 1760s. The cabinetmaker Carlin specialised in this kind of furniture, decorated with delicate floral porcelain panels. This desk was probably commissioned by the prominent luxury goods dealers Simon-Philippe Poirier and Dominique Daguerre. The floral swag mounts along the frieze of the desk and the elegant tapering legs are typical of the Neoclassical style. The rich pink and purple colours of the wood veneers, now faded, would once have matched some of the bright colours on the porcelain plaques. The central apron-shaped plaque at the bottom imitates a fringed drape of the form found in French interiors of the late 17th century.

Roll-top desk, about 1770

Jean-Henri Riesener (1734–1806)

H. 139 cm | Inv. no. F102

One of Riesener's earliest major works, this magnificent desk was supplied to the twenty-one-year-old comte d'Orsay, a member of a leading family of financiers and tax farmers. It is very similar to the roll-top desk made for Louis XV of France by Jean-François Oeben and Riesener, which was delivered just a year or so earlier, but it has been tailored for the young aristocrat: on each side the coloured marquetry includes his cipher, *ORS*. Other elements may also refer to d'Orsay himself. For example, the dove carrying a letter on the roll-top may allude to his marriage in 1770, and the military trophies on the sides may allude to his commission as a captain of dragoons.

The Grand Turk giving a Concert to his Mistress, 1727

Carle van Loo (1705–1765)

H. 72.5 x W. 91 cm | Inv. no. P451

This scene is an early example of the 18th-century fascination with *turquerie.* A contemporary resonance has been added by the artist's depiction of his wife, the opera singer Cristina Antonia Somis, known to contemporaries as the 'Philomel of Turin'. She sings a fashionable aria of the day, 'Si caro, si', from George Frideric Handel's opera *Admeto.* The painting was exhibited at the Paris Salon of 1737, together with a related work, *The Grand Turk having his Mistress Painted,* in which Van Loo portrayed himself as the artist. The two paintings thus celebrate the complementary talents of Van Loo and his wife.

STUDY

FRANCE IN THE AGE OF MARIE-ANTOINETTE

The Study is dedicated to taste in the period of Marie-Antoinette, Queen of France. An exceptional group of furniture owned by the queen is surrounded by Sèvres porcelain and other French decorative arts from the second half of the 18th century, when a renewed preoccupation with the art of ancient Greece and Rome took hold. The paintings of Jean-Honoré Fragonard, Jean-Baptiste Greuze and Élisabeth-Louise Vigée Le Brun mark the same transition.

The Study was Sir Richard Wallace's private room for writing letters and reading. The photograph below, taken about 1888, shows that he had the room hung with watercolours, while an impressive Boulle wardrobe was flanked by marble busts of Sir Richard's wife, Lady Wallace, and his likely father, the 4th Marquess of Hertford.

The Study, about 1888.

The Swing, 1767

Jean-Honoré Fragonard
(1732–1806)
H. 81 x W. 64.2 cm |
Inv. no. P430

Breathtaking in its sense of freedom, movement and romance, this is Fragonard's most famous work, and indeed, one of the most emblematic images of 18th-century art. Its genesis was reported by an 18th-century source. A prominent painter of religious scenes was initially approached by an unnamed aristocrat to paint his young mistress on a swing. Not wishing to jeopardise his reputation, the religious painter refused but suggested Fragonard. The latter's acceptance of this unconventional commission marked his decisive break away from the rarefied 'official' art world in favour of the freedom and personal choice afforded by the private art market.

Tea service, 1779

Sèvres Manufactory

Various dimensions | Inv. nos C407–13

C407

This tea service is one of the few examples of Sèvres hard-paste porcelain in the Collection (most is soft paste). The fanciful decoration is in keeping with the taste for whimsical visions of China, known as *chinoiserie*, but a direct source for the motifs has not been identified. It is the work of Louis-François Lécot, a painter who specialised in *chinoiserie* decoration on hard-paste porcelain. This type of decoration was fashionable at Sèvres in the 1770s. Tea sets such as this are known to have been in the collections of Louis XVI of France and the duchesse de Mazarin, and the lavish decoration and rich gilding on this one certainly suggest that it would have been bought by an extremely wealthy individual.

Madame Perregaux, 1789

Élisabeth-Louise Vigée Le Brun (1755–1842)

H. 99.6 x W. 78.5 cm | Inv. no. P457

Made by one of the rare female artists represented in the Collection, this painting depicts Adélaïde de Praël, wife of banker Jean-François Perregaux, who would eventually count among his clients the 3rd Marquess of Hertford. It is signed and dated 1789, making it one of the last works Vigée Le Brun painted before she left France. The artist, a prominent society portraitist best known for her close association with Marie-Antoinette, correctly gaged the changing political mood and emigrated just in time to escape oncoming revolution.

This splendid garniture of vases is decorated with jewelled enamelling applied over a deep blue ground. A particularly difficult technique, the jewelled decoration was only carried out for a few years at Sèvres. On their fronts, the vases are painted with mythological scenes from Ovid's *Metamorphoses* after compositions by François Boucher and Charles Eisen: *Pygmalion and Galatea* on the central vase and *Primavera with two Cherubs* and *Bacchus accompanied by two Child Satyrs* on the vases on either side. Sèvres pieces decorated using this rare and costly technique were often given by Louis XVI of France as diplomatic gifts. This garniture, originally probably bought by Marie-Antoinette, was later presented by the king to Prince Heinrich of Prussia during a diplomatic visit to Paris in 1784.

Garniture of three vases and covers, 1781

Sèvres Manufactory
H. 47.5 cm (C334), H. 39.3 cm (C335) and H. 38.9 cm (C336) | Inv. nos C334–6

Fall-front desk, 1783

Jean-Henri Riesener (1734–1806)
H. 139.6 cm | Inv. no. F302

Marie-Antoinette escaped the rigours of court etiquette by visiting the Petit Trianon, a small but perfectly formed house in the grounds of the Palace of Versailles that became her personal retreat. Both she and her husband, Louis XVI of France, had apartments there and she was involved in choosing the furniture for their rooms. This desk, with a fall-front that hides several small drawers and pigeon-holes and drops down to provide a writing surface, was supplied to the Petit Trianon by Riesener, her favourite cabinetmaker, on 8 March 1783. It was intended for her boudoir, a small room connecting to both her bedroom and the salon, leading directly out into the grounds.

Perfume burner, 1773–5

Gilt-bronze mounts by Pierre Gouthière (1732–1813)

H. 48.3 cm | Inv. no. F292

The gilt-bronze mounts of this perfume burner represent the finest work of Gouthière, the leading maker of gilt bronzes in France before the Revolution. It was made for the duc d'Aumont, first gentleman of the king's bedchamber, and was acquired at the sale of his collection in 1782 by Marie-Antoinette. Perfume burners of this kind were modelled on the bronze tripods featured in wall paintings at Pompeii and Herculaneum and in Roman decoration. The bowl of this example is made of red jasper, probably cut in the workshop set up by the duc d'Aumont in the Hôtel des Menus-Plaisirs, which housed the department of the French royal household responsible for organising celebrations and ceremonies.

The Souvenir, **1776–8**

Jean-Honoré Fragonard (1732–1806)

H. 25.2 x W. 19 cm | Inv. no. P382

A young girl, identified in a sale catalogue of 1792 as Jean-Jacques Rousseau's heroine Julie, carves an initial into the bark of a tree, while being observed by her pet spaniel, the symbol of her fidelity. The theme reflects the increasing preoccupation with human emotion during the second half of the 18th century. Its scale and careful technique also show Fragonard varying his style to echo the contemporary taste for the 'little masters' of the Dutch Republic, although he continued to animate such stylistic references with his own theatrical lighting, delicate draughtsmanship and calligraphic traceries of hair and foliage.

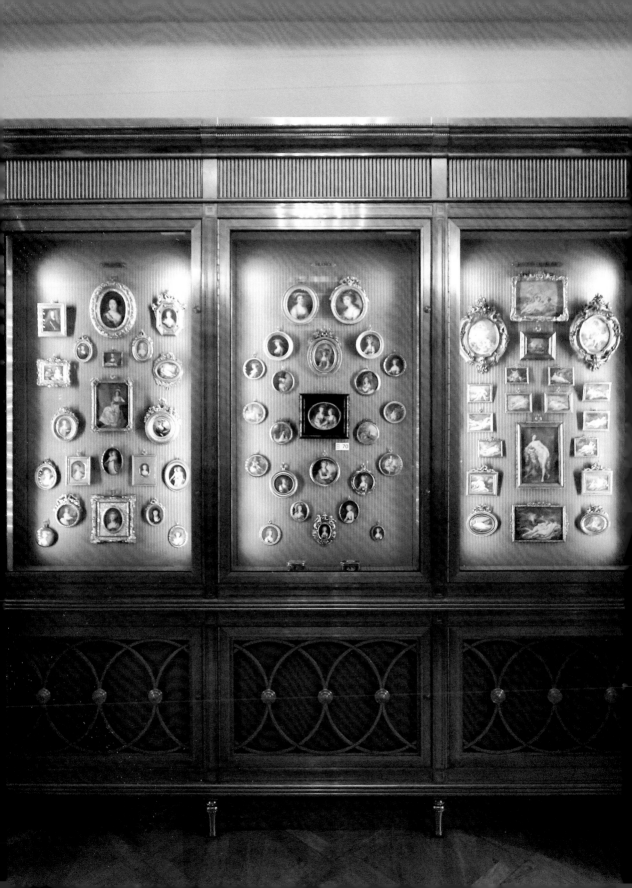

BOUDOIR CABINET

GOLD BOXES AND MINIATURES

This cabinet room houses the miniature arts of the 17th and 18th centuries, with miniature paintings, gold boxes and other luxury objects. Miniatures had a strong personal and emotional significance. They could serve as souvenirs of favourite places or important events. Portrait miniatures were given as a sign of love or friendship and kept by their owners as tokens of attachment or political allegiance. Miniatures also served as a medium for pornography. Gold boxes, usually used for snuff, were extravagant possessions that reflected the latest fashion in shape, materials and decoration. They are both small and intensely personal objects, yet they also represent a microcosm of the arts of 18th-century France.

Miniatures displayed in the Oval Drawing Room, about 1888.

Maria Cosway, about 1785–90

Richard Cosway (1742–1821)

H. 7.1 x W. 5.8 cm | Inv. no. M87

Richard Cosway married Maria Hadfield in 1781. She had moved to London in 1779 after growing up in an English expatriate family in Florence. In England, she became an important painter in her own right, an accomplished musician and, together with her husband, the centre of a highly fashionable circle. The Cosways were celebrities of their day, famous both as artists and as society figures. Their stormy relationship and affairs increased the public interest in them. Maria Cosway spent most of her life from 1790 in France and Italy and was effectively separated from her husband, although they still lived together at times and never lost touch. The turban that Maria Cosway is wearing in the portrait was at the height of fashion in the late 1780s.

Snuffbox, about 1775 (miniatures probably later)

Dresden, Germany, probably Johann Christian Neuber (1736–1808)

W. 8.3 cm | Inv. no. G80

Neuber is one of the most celebrated goldsmiths of 18th-century Dresden, noted particularly for his work with hardstones. This oval box by Neuber comprises plaques of carnelian, set within a delicate gold trellis. The carnelian panel on the lid is carved in relief with a depiction of Leda and the Swan, probably by an anonymous Dresden lapidary. A secret slide can be revealed by pressing on a part of the box that contains two miniature portraits, mounted back-to-back, of the writer Voltaire and the mathematician Madame du Châtelet, who had a celebrated liaison. These have been added to the box later.

The Painter's Family, 1776

Peter Adolf Hall (1739–1793)
H. 8.9 x W. 10.9 cm | Inv. no. M186

Born in Sweden, Hall trained with the pastelist Gustav Lundberg before moving to Paris and becoming the leading miniaturist of his day. Generally regarded as his masterpiece, this miniature reveals how much of his appeal lay in his scintillating technique, decorative palette and idealising approach. It depicts his wife, Adélaïde, her sister, the comtesse de Serre, and his eldest daughter, Adélaïde-Victorine, then four years old. The charming family group, with the young mother embracing her child and sister, reflects the new mood of sensibility made fashionable in the French capital by the writings of Jean-Jacques Rousseau and the paintings of Jean-Baptiste Greuze.

Snuffbox, 1781–3

Pierre-François Drais
(1726–1788), miniatures
by Henri-Joseph van
Blarenberghe (1741–1826)
W. 8.6 cm | Inv. no. G62

This gold box features six glorious miniatures by Van Blarenberghe with views of the Château de Romainville, near Paris. The box and its miniatures were commissioned by the owner of this estate, the marquis de Ségur, who was minister of war to Louis XVI of France in 1780. Ségur himself appears on the lid, where we see the château behind a village festival known as the *Rosière*. This ceremony, during which a village girl would be crowned with a wreath of roses and presented with her dowry, came to epitomise certain 18th-century ideas of natural virtue and pastoral idylls. The box is the only one in the Collection whose original patron is personally identified.

Marguerite Gérard, 1793

François Dumont (1751–1831)

H. 15.8 x W. 11.8 cm | Inv. no. M101

Dumont, who became an associate
member of the Royal Academy in 1788
and a regular exhibiter at the Paris
Salon from 1789 until 1827, was the
most successful miniaturist in Paris
following the death of Peter Adolf Hall.
This miniature, typical of Dumont's
most brilliant period, depicts the
painter Marguerite Gérard, who was
the pupil of Jean-Honoré Fragonard.
The restricted palette and relaxed pose
of the sitter in front of a scumbled
(blurred) background reflected recent
developments in contemporary
portraiture by Jacques-Louis David and
Élisabeth-Louise Vigée Le Brun.

Snuffbox, 1744

Jean Ducrollay (about 1710–1787)

W. 7.6 cm | Inv. no. G4

This superb box, made in Paris by
perhaps the finest snuffbox maker
of 18th-century France, Ducrollay,
resembles a scallop shell and is
enamelled as a white peacock's
fantail in full display on the cover.
Anyone standing opposite the
owner of this box would therefore
have the impression of the peacock
displaying his tail when the
owner lifted the lid. The box was
owned by the duc d'Aumont, first
gentleman of Louis XV of France's
bedchamber, until his death in 1782.

BOUDOIR

SENSIBILITY AND THE SUBLIME

The paintings in the Boudoir by Jean-Baptiste Greuze, Joshua Reynolds and Claude-Joseph Vernet are important examples of the new interest in strong emotions that developed in European art in the 1760s. The visual arts expressed this change even earlier than literature. In this room, paintings are shown alongside French furniture from the 1760s and later in the 18th century.

In Sir Richard and Lady Wallace's time, the room was a boudoir or private sitting room that housed small paintings, Sèvres porcelain and Renaissance jewellery.

The Boudoir, about 1890.

Filing-cabinet, writing-table and inkstand, about 1765

René Dubois (1737–1798)
H. 214.1 cm (F178), H. 75.4 cm (F330) and H. 15.3 cm
(F287) | Inv. nos F178, F330 and F287

This suite of furniture by Dubois is one of the most important early examples of Neoclassicism in France. Striking for its green-coloured lacquered finish, the furniture is also dominated by gilt-bronze mounts. The filing-cabinet is surmounted by a gilt-bronze group depicting the nymph Psyche embracing Cupid, and below are figures representing Peace and War. The writing-table is dominated by the sinuous gilt-bronze sirens placed at each corner, their tails intertwining with the table legs. The suite may have been designed by Charles de Wailly, an architect at the forefront of the Neoclassical movement.

A Storm with a Shipwreck, 1754

Claude-Joseph Vernet (1714–1789)
H. 87 x W. 137 cm | Inv. no. P135

Commissioned by Madame de Pompadour's brother, the marquis de Marigny, after he had become minister for the arts under Louis XV of France, this picture was painted in Marseille, where Vernet lived between October 1753 and September 1754. Shipwrecks were a favourite subject of the artist, allowing him to invest his seascapes with dramatic emotional content.

This scene demonstrates man's helplessness in the face of nature. According to some contemporary critics, including the philosopher Denis Diderot, the excellence of Vernet's figure drawing and his mastery of gesture and expression elevated such works to the realm of the admired genre of history painting.

Miss Jane Bowles, 1775–6
Joshua Reynolds (1723–1792)
H. 91 x W. 70.9 cm | Inv. no. P36

Jane Bowles was the eldest child of Oldfield Bowles of North Aston in Oxfordshire, an amateur painter of some distinction. When deciding which painter to employ to paint his daughter, Bowles invited Reynolds to dinner to see how he got on with his potential subject. According to Reynolds's 19th-century biographer, C.R. Leslie, 'The little girl was placed next to Sir Joshua at the dessert, where he amused her so much with stories and tricks that she thought him the most charming man in the world ... The next day she was delighted to be taken to his house, where she sat down with a face full of glee, the expression of which he caught at once and never lost'.

The Broken Mirror, 1762–3
Jean-Baptiste Greuze (1725–1805)
H. 56 x W. 45.6 cm | Inv. no. P442

A fine example of Greuze's modern, moral genre subjects, *The Broken Mirror* is a parable of carelessness, where the chaotic state of the interior and the girl's dress reflect the disarray of her morals. The fact that the girl, who laments the loss of her virginity, is unmarried is emphasised by the yapping dog, a common symbol of desire in 18th-century French painting, and her ringless hand, which draws our attention as it is positioned in the centre of the picture. The painting belonged to François Boucher's friend and patron, Paul Randon de Boisset, who liked it so much that he refused to lend it to the Paris Salon of 1763.

WEST ROOM

BRITISH PORTRAITS OF THE 18TH CENTURY

This room contains masterpieces of 18th-century British portraiture. All the sitters are women. Three portraits are of Mrs Robinson, a famous actress of the period. Her striking full-length portrait by Thomas Gainsborough hangs with smaller works by Joshua Reynolds and George Romney. Reynolds's work is also showcased in a number of other portraits, including that of the courtesan Nelly O'Brien, which is widely regarded as one of his most original and accomplished compositions.

The mantel clock modelled after Michelangelo Buonarroti's figures of Night and Day in Florence, and the elaborate silver-gilt toilet service from Augsburg, herald a transition from France to a wider Europe in the following sequence of galleries.

Formerly Sir Richard and Lady Wallace's Bedroom, upholstered in blue and white, this room contained Sèvres porcelain, French furniture and paintings, including Jean-Honoré Fragonard's *Swing*.

The West Room, 1958.

The Augsburg Service, 1767–73

Germany, various silversmiths | Inv. nos W225–78

Toilet services were an integral part of the morning ritual at which wealthy members of society were prepared for the day while receiving favoured guests. The German city of Augsburg became the leading centre of the production of these services. As luxury objects that advertised the owner's wealth and status,

they became highly elaborate and costly. This service, in the mature German Rococo style, is one of the largest to survive. It contains fifty-five pieces for both the toilet and the breakfast meal. There are various boxes, a mirror, coffee and tea pots and even an inkstand with a bell that was used to call a servant.

Mantel clock, about 1775

Movement attributed to either Jean-André Lepaute
(1720–1788) or Jean-Baptiste Lepaute (1727–1801)
H. 68 cm | Inv. no. F268

The design of this clock is attributed to the architect Antoine-Mathieu Le Carpentier, who worked with Jean-André Lepaute on a similar clock delivered to the prince de Condé's gallery at the Palais-Bourbon in Paris in 1772. The figures of Night and Day are based on marble statues made by Michelangelo Buonarroti for the tomb of Giuliano de' Medici in Florence. These figures were first used on clocks by André-Charles Boulle. The Neoclassical movement, which was well underway by 1775, not only looked back to Classical Antiquity directly but also through the prisms of the Renaissance and French 17th-century Classicism, making the works of Boulle a popular source of inspiration.

Chest-of-drawers, about 1765

Attributed to René Dubois (1737–1798)
H. 93 cm | Inv. no. F245

In the past, this chest-of-drawers has been associated with both Madame de Pompadour and Marie-Antoinette, but neither link has been verified. It is possible, however, that Pompadour may have commissioned it just before she died and never took delivery of it. Intended to stand below a pier glass, it is veneered with three separate panels of high-quality Japanese lacquer overlaid in part by a matted, gilt-bronze, Chinese-style fret. By contrast, the gilt-bronze sirens supporting tasselled cushions on their heads are a much more European feature. This combination of elements is typical of the more avant-garde, luxury French furniture of this period.

Mrs Mary Robinson ('Perdita'), 1781

Thomas Gainsborough (1727–1788)
H. 233.7 x W. 153 cm |
Inv. no. P42

The seventeen-year-old prince of Wales (later George IV of the United Kingdom) became infatuated with Mrs Robinson in 1779 after seeing her as Perdita in William Shakespeare's *The Winter's Tale* at the Drury Lane Theatre in London. 'Perdita', as she was thereafter nicknamed, became his first mistress. Towards the end of 1780, the prince abandoned her for a rival, and she spent the following eight months struggling to persuade him to honour his obligations. Following a financial settlement, relations between the former lovers again became cordial and the prince commissioned this portrait. Gainsborough's masterful handling and the marriage of pose and landscape impart a characteristic poetic dimension to the painting.

Miss Nelly O'Brien, about 1762–4

Joshua Reynolds (1723–1792)
H. 126.3 x W. 101 cm | Inv. no. P38

Nelly O'Brien was a courtesan and a friend of Reynolds. She sat for his 'fancy pictures' and numerous portraits. This experimental work, which is a combination of the two pictorial types, was probably not commissioned but rather intended primarily for public display at exhibition. The artist demonstrates his great ability in depicting the different textures and delicate colour harmonies of the sitter's costume, as well as the luminous effects of shadow and reflected light on her face and bosom. The painting was much admired by contemporaries and frequently engraved.

Mrs Mary Robinson ('Perdita'), 1780–81

George Romney (1734–1802)
H. 75.7 x W. 63.2 cm | Inv. no. P37

Romney presents Robinson in a fairly plain but fashionable costume (this is in direct contrast to Gainsborough's portrait of the sitter opposite, which alludes to her celebrity). The facial expression is also notable, as she raises one eyebrow, as if tempting the viewer to challenge her. Romney exhibited the painting at the Royal Academy exhibition in 1782 and had it engraved by J.R. Smith; it was sufficiently well known for it to be used as the basis for a caricature of the sitter in 1783. The portrait remained in the artist's possession until his death and was bought for twenty guineas at his sale by the 2nd Marquess of Hertford.

WEST GALLERY I

VENETIAN VIEW PAINTING

Giovanni Antonio Canal, called Canaletto, and Francesco Guardi were the two outstanding Venetian view painters of the 18th century. Although Canaletto's style seems much more descriptive than Guardi's, both artists created a carefully staged image of Venice. Most of their works were painted for tourists visiting the city, primarily British travellers who came to the Venetian Republic on their Grand Tour. Like many of these tourists, the 1st Marquess of Hertford acquired paintings by Canaletto, perhaps to remind him of his time in Italy. They are among the earliest acquisitions of works of art by the family to remain in the Collection.

This gallery was created in 1897 from Sir Richard Wallace's Dressing Room, Lady Wallace's Bathroom and Dressing Room and a corridor.

The West Gallery, about 1900.

Venice: the Riva degli Schiavoni* and *Venice: the Molo with Santa Maria della Salute, about 1740–45

Giovanni Antonio Canal, called Canaletto (1697–1768)

H. 58.2 x W. 93.5 cm (P509) and H. 57.7 x W. 93.5 cm (P516) | Inv. nos P509 and P516

These paintings constitute iconic views of Venice's waterfront from opposite directions of the promenade, or Riva degli Schiavoni, with gondolas bobbing on the water before the Doge's Palace. In *The Riva degli Schiavoni*, the columns of St Theodore and St Mark are visible at the entrance to the Ponte della Paglia and prison beyond. *The Molo with Santa Maria della Salute* is framed by the Doge's Palace on the right, looking across the Piazzetta and the library, towards the mouth of the Grand Canal with the church of Santa Maria della Salute and the Dogana, or customs house, on the opposite bank. The Giudecca, with the church of the Redentore, are visible on the left.

Two of the most important churches in 18th-century Venice feature in these paintings. *San Giorgio Maggiore with the Giudecca and the Zitelle* shows a view across the Bacino di San Marco, looking towards the church of San Giorgio Maggiore. The view is taken from the quayside of the mainland (the Riva degli Schiavoni) and represents one of the most popular scenes within 18th-century Venetian view painting. *Santa Maria della Salute and the Dogana* shows a view across the Grand Canal, looking towards the church of Santa Maria della Salute. These paintings are not topographically accurate, and the views have been manipulated. This is characteristic of Guardi's later work, in which the artist often enlarged spaces or rearranged buildings for artistic effect.

Venice: San Giorgio Maggiore with the Giudecca and the Zitelle and **Venice: Santa Maria della Salute and the Dogana, 1780s**

Francesco Guardi (1712–1793)
H. 68.7 x W. 91.5 cm (P491) and H. 68.5 x W. 90.5 cm (P503) |
Inv. nos P491 and P503

This splendid inkstand was made in the Valadier workshop in the via del Babuino, Rome, for Pope Pius VI. Valadier was a highly talented designer, goldsmith and bronzeworker, whose workshop produced decorative art objects for many of the European elite. The five containers consist of a central pen holder in the shape of a vase of serpentine marble supported on a pedestal, a sand shaker and inkwell, both in the form of cylindrical pedestals, and two sarcophagus-shaped containers supported on lion-paw feet. The stand is decorated with gilt-bronze eagles and cameos of classical male heads, including Homer, Socrates and Julius Caesar.

Inkstand, about 1785

Luigi Valadier (1726–1785)
H. 26.5 cm | Inv. no. F288

Chair, about 1730

Design attributed to William Kent (1685–1748)
H. 96.3 cm | Inv. no. F462

Of the same model as four armchairs at Chatsworth House, it is believed that this chair was part of a set made to designs by the painter, architect and designer Kent for the 3rd Earl of Burlington's newly built Chiswick House. Eight armchairs were inventoried in the Blue Velvet Room at Chiswick in 1770; they stood against the walls of the room, which were hung with landscape paintings and British portraits. The design is characteristic of the bold, sculptural forms employed by Kent on much of his furniture and reflects the ideas he assimilated from his visits to Italy.

Please
lift covers

WEST GALLERY II

RICHARD PARKES BONINGTON AND EUGÈNE DELACROIX

This display, created in 2010, houses paintings by the brilliant generation of British and French painters who came to maturity during the 1820s. After thirty years of turbulence in France, culminating in the collapse of the Napoleonic Empire, many painters began to seek new inspiration from earlier European history and legend, as well as literature, which offered an alternative to the Classicism promoted by the French academic system.

When Sir Richard and Lady Wallace lived at Hertford House, this space was occupied by part of the European arms and armour collection.

The West Gallery, about 1888.

Henri IV and the Spanish Ambassador, **1827**
Richard Parkes Bonington (1802–1828)
H. 38.4 x W. 52.4 cm | Inv. no. P351

This painting was exhibited at the Paris Salon of 1827–8. The subject is taken from an apocryphal anecdote in the *Mémorial pittoresque de la France,* published in 1786, concerning Henri IV of France. It recalled how the king, one of the most able and popular of French monarchs, was playing with the dauphin (the heir to the French throne) in his chambers at the Palace of Fontainebleau in 1604, letting him ride on his back, when an ambassador arrived 'to discover the conqueror of the Catholic League and the Monarch of France in this undignified position'. Henri, without getting up, stopped and asked, 'have you any children, Ambassador?', to which the envoy replied, 'yes, Sire'. Henri, continuing to play with his son, retorted, 'then I may finish my trip around the room'.

The Execution of the Doge Marino Faliero,
1825–6

Eugène Delacroix (1798–1863)
H. 145.6 x W. 113.8 cm | Inv. no. P282

When Delacroix painted this picture, one of his own favourite works, he was briefly sharing a studio with Richard Parkes Bonington. The influence of his English friend can be seen in the colouring and the bold execution of the figures. The subject is taken from Lord Byron's tragedy *Marino Faliero, Doge of Venice.* Faliero was elected doge in 1354 but was executed the following year after conspiring against the Venetian state. The setting recalls the Giant's Staircase in the Doge's Palace, while the costumes, some of the heads of the dignitaries and the rich colouring are derived from Venetian Renaissance painting, which Delacroix greatly admired.

Fall-front desk, about 1777

Pierre-Antoine Foullet (master 1765)

H. 149 cm | Inv. no. F299

Unusually, this fall-front desk bears the signature in marquetry of the cabinetmaker who made it – Foullet. The pictorial marquetry is characteristic of work by him. It depicts a scene of classical architecture, some of it in ruins, against a landscape of trees and sky. Originally, this would have been very colourful, with the sky a deep blue made from stained sycamore. The marquetry in the bottom section includes a basket of roses, a floral swag and two classical trophies depicting attributes of war and engineering. The gilt-bronze mounts, which include two helmeted cuirasses (body armours) supporting a shield with a coat of arms, and a lion's head evoking the might of Hercules, emphasise the military association.

Edward V and the Duke of York in the Tower, 1831

Hippolyte (Paul) Delaroche (1797–1856)

H. 43.5 x W. 51.3 cm | Inv. no. P276

This is a replica of a much larger painting exhibited at the Paris Salon of 1831, which is now in the Musée du Louvre, Paris. The subject is probably taken from Act 4, Scene 3, of William Shakespeare's *Richard III*. Edward V of England, who succeeded to the throne on the death of his father, Edward IV, was deposed by his uncle, the Duke of Gloucester (later Richard III), on 22 June 1483. Shortly afterwards, Edward and his younger brother, the Duke of York, were murdered in the Tower of London. Fittingly, this painting, with its stage-like setting and melodramatic subject, is highly theatrical. The dog and perhaps the young Duke of York sense the arrival of the approaching murderers. An ominous shadow can be seen at the bottom of the door to the bedchamber.

WEST GALLERY III

19TH-CENTURY PAINTINGS AND NAPOLEONICA

This gallery is hung densely, as was customary in Sir Richard and
Lady Wallace's day, with paintings by fashionable 19th-century
artists, including Alexandre-Gabriel Decamps, Hippolyte (Paul)
Delaroche, Louise-Eugène-Gabriel Isabey and Horace Vernet.
Many of these painters, such as (Jean-Louis-) Ernest Meissonier,
belonged to the artistic and literary salon society of 19th-century
Paris and were contemporaries and, in some cases, friends of
the 4th Marquess of Hertford and Sir Richard. Hertford's strong
interest in Napoleon I, Emperor of the French, can be seen in the
large collection of works of art illustrating the emperor and his life.

During Sir Richard and Lady Wallace's lifetime, this room housed
part of the European arms and armour collection.

West Gallery III, about 1888.

Francesca da Rimini, 1835

Ary Scheffer (1795-1858)

H. 166.5 x W. 234 cm | Inv. no. P316

Scheffer enjoyed enormous success with sentimental and religious scenes, many of which became the subject of popular engravings. *Francesca da Rimini* was one of his most admired works; this is the first version. A subject from Dante Alighieri's *Inferno*, the composition shows Dante and his guide, the Roman poet Virgil, during their passage through Hell. They look on the tragic figures of Paolo and Francesca, condemned with the souls of the lustful to the stormy darkness of Hell's second circle. Francesca was forced to marry the hideous Gianciotto da Rimini but fell in love with his handsome younger brother, Paolo. In 1285, they were murdered by Gianciotto after he saw Paolo kiss Francesca while they were reading an account of the love of Sir Lancelot for Queen Guinevere.

Polichinelle, 1860

(Jean-Louis-) Ernest Meissonier (1815–1891)
H. 55.2 x W. 36 cm | Inv. no. P337

With his baggy trousers, large belly and characteristic wooden clogs, the jolly Polichinelle (or Punch, as he is better known in English) is unmistakable. This representation of the popular character from the *commedia dell'arte* was originally painted on a door panel in the Paris apartment owned by Apollonie Sabatier. A celebrated artists' muse, her famous Paris salon attracted all the prominent French artists of the 19th century, including Gustave Doré, Victor Hugo and Édouard Manet, among others. She was also the long-time mistress of Sir Richard Wallace.

Napoleon I, 1810

Jean-Baptiste Isabey (1767–1855)
H. 21.5 x W. 17 cm | Inv. no. M232

Isabey, who first worked for Marie-Antoinette, was adept at securing patronage from the varied political systems in power in France during his long life. Under Napoleon I, Emperor of the French, he rose to become court painter, providing, with the help of a large studio, countless miniatures of the emperor and his extensive family. This is actually a sepia drawing rather than a miniature, but it shows the high quality of draughtsmanship of which Isabey was capable. Napoleon wears robes of state as well as a laurel wreath and the collar of the Legion of Honour. One of Isabey's duties had been to design the costumes for Napoleon's coronation in 1804.

Napoleon's Tomb, 1821

Horace Vernet (1789-1863)

H. 54 x W. 80.5 cm | Inv. no. P575

When Vernet learned in July 1821 that Napoleon I, Emperor of the French, had died in May, he immediately set out to paint a heroic burial scene paying homage to the emperor. Napoleon's tomb on the island of St Helena is surrounded by mourning generals and resurrected marshals, with the wreckage of a ship inscribed with the names of his most important battles floating in the waves below. The kneeling, turbaned figure is a member of Napoleon's esteemed Mamluk regiment. This romantic visualisation of Napoleon's death was to become the first of many scenes that would transform Napoleon into a fallen hero and martyr.

Sheep in the Highlands, 1857

Rosa Bonheur (1822-1899)

H. 46 x W. 65 cm | Inv. no. P364

Although largely self-taught, Bonheur became the leading French animal painter of her time and the first woman to receive the Legion of Honour. Her works, which owe much to her careful study of Dutch animal paintings in the Musée du Louvre, Paris, are characterised by an unsentimental naturalism derived from close observation. In 1856, she made a triumphant tour of England and Scotland at the invitation of the dealer Ernest Gambart. *Sheep in the Highlands* was probably inspired by observations made during this trip, when she was profoundly impressed by the beauty and historical associations of the Scottish Highlands.

Macbeth, paysage (Macbeth, Landscape), 1858–9

Jean-Baptiste-Camille Corot
(1796–1875)
H. 111 x W. 135.7 cm | Inv. no. P281

Begun in 1858, this ambitious representation of a scene from William Shakespeare's *Macbeth* was exhibited at the Paris Salon the following year. It depicts the moment at which Macbeth and Banquo, generals of King Duncan, meet three witches, who predict Macbeth's rise to the Scottish throne. The scene unfolds at the edge of a forest, where Macbeth and Banquo are almost hidden in the shade; the figures of the three witches are silhouetted against the bright sky. Corot shows one of the witches pointing at the two men. The young Claude Monet greatly admired Corot's painting when he saw it at the salon. After the Collection opened its doors to the public in 1900, this became one of the most popular works in the new museum.

GREAT GALLERY

The Great Gallery was built in 1872–5 as part of an extension to Hertford House, when Sir Richard Wallace moved an important part of his collection from Paris to London. An imposing room with large areas of uninterrupted wall space and natural top light, it has always been the gallery where many of the greatest paintings in the Collection have been displayed alongside furniture and sculpture.

The Great Gallery now unites many of the most important 17th-century paintings from the Dutch Republic, Flanders, France, Italy and Spain, reflecting the international character and lively artistic exchange between the major European artistic centres during the Baroque age. With works by Philippe de Champaigne, Nicolas Poussin, Rembrandt van Rijn, Peter Paul Rubens, Diego Velázquez and many of their contemporaries in one room, it offers a unique panorama of art of the highest quality.

Sir Richard conceived this superb space, the largest and most magnificent room at Hertford House, as being the culmination of any visit to his collection.

The Great Gallery, about 1888.

Canaletto excelled at painting topographical views of his native Venice that were popular with Grand Tourists during the 18th century. This extremely fine pair of views depicts the Bacino di San Marco from opposing vantage points. In the first painting, the viewer is placed on the steps of the church of San Giorgio Maggiore looking across the Bacino di San Marco towards the Canale della Giudecca on the left, with the opening of the Grand Canal in the centre of the canvas, and the Campanile (bell tower), the Piazzetta and the Doge's Palace on the right. The second painting looks towards the Church of San Giorgio Maggiore, with the Riva degli Schiavoni in the background on the left. The Dogana (customs house) frames the composition on the left.

Venice: the Bacino di San Marco from San Giorgio Maggiore **and**
Venice: the Bacino di San Marco from the Canale della Giudecca,
about 1735–44

Giovanni Antonio Canal, called Canaletto (1697–1768)
H. 129.2 x W. 188.9 cm (P497) and H. 130.2 x W. 190.8 cm (P499)
| Inv. nos P497 and P499

The Laughing Cavalier, **1624**
Frans Hals (1582/3–1666)
H. 83 x W. 67.3 cm | Inv. no. P84

A highly gifted portraitist, Hals had a supreme ability to characterise his sitters and bring them to life. This exuberant portrait of a man, aged 26 and wearing the latest French fashions, is Hals's most famous painting and one of the most iconic pictures in the history of Western art. The man's confident pose, with his left hand on his hip, coupled with his direct, penetrating gaze, imbue the portrait with a unique vitality. The black cloak is particularly noteworthy as it showcases Hals's dazzling capacity to paint convincingly using a limited colour palette, leading Vincent van Gogh to exclaim that 'Frans Hals must have had 27 blacks'.

Hercules overcoming the Centaur Eurytion and Hercules overcoming Acheloüs in the form of a Bull, about 1640–50

S118: Model by Pietro Tacca (1577–1640), after a design by Giovanni da Bologna, called Giambologna (1529–1608), and cast by Ferdinando Tacca (1619–1686)
S124: Model by Pietro Tacca and cast by Ferdinando Tacca
H. 67 cm (S118) and H. 58.4 cm (S124) | Inv. nos S118 and S124

This pair of bronzes, depicting episodes from the Labours of Hercules, is a splendid representation of Baroque dynamism, movement, strength and three-dimensional design. The first sculpture shows the hero battling with the centaur Eurytion, who was about to forcefully marry King Dexamenos's daughter, sometimes identified as Deianira. Hercules intervened and killed the creature. The second sculpture shows Hercules's struggle with the river god Acheloüs, another of Hercules's rivals for the hand of Deianira. Acheloüs transformed himself into a bull, but Hercules defeated him by ripping off one of his horns, which became the cornucopia, the classical symbol of abundance.

Chest-of-drawers, about 1786

Attributed to Johann Gottlob Fiedler (active 1775–86)
H. 89 cm | Inv. no. F521

Fiedler was based in Berlin and made furniture for the Prussian court. His clients included Friedrich Wilhelm II, who acceded to the Prussian throne in 1786, and Prince Heinrich of Prussia, Friedrich II's younger brother. This chest-of-drawers is in a Neoclassical manner and stylistically similar to others that are known to have been made for the king's apartments at the Berlin Palace after it was remodelled by Friedrich Wilhelm von Erdmannsdorff. It is very unusual to find a German piece of furniture in the Collection, but it appears to have been attributed to the celebrated Parisian cabinetmaker Jean-Henri Riesener in the 19th century.

Joseph and his Brethren, **about 1665–70**

Bartolomé Esteban Murillo (1617–1682)
H. 151.9 x W. 225.6 cm | Inv. no. P46

The subject of this painting sets it apart from the other Murillos in the Collection, both as a scene from the Old Testament and as a depiction of strong emotions. According to the Book of Genesis, Joseph was the favourite son of his father, Jacob, and much envied by his elder brothers. When he appeared to his brothers wearing a new coat of many colours given to him by his father, they resolved to kill him due to their jealousy. Murillo depicts the moment when Joseph's brother Reuben persuaded the others to mitigate the crime by abandoning the boy in an empty well. The 4th Marquess of Hertford was at first unsure whether to purchase the painting due to the unsettling subject.

River Landscape with Apollo and the Cumaean Sibyl, **about 1657–8**

Salvator Rosa (1615–1673)
H. 173.7 x W. 259.5 cm | Inv. no. P116

In Ovid's *Metamorphoses*, the amorous Apollo offered the Cumaean Sibyl anything she desired. She is depicted here asking for as many years of life as there are grains of dust in her hands. Although Apollo granted her wish, she still refused him any favours. In retribution, he denied her perpetual youth and she lived for a thousand years in misery. Rosa's expressive brushwork, dark tones and dramatic *chiaroscuro* (strong contrasts between light and dark), together with his characterisation of the wild, rocky landscape with splintered trees, create a sense of foreboding and mystery in keeping with the melancholic story.

Chest-of-drawers, about 1695

Attributed to Alexandre-Jean Oppenordt (1639–1715)
H. 87.5 cm | Inv. no. F405

Magnificent, sarcophagus-shaped chests-of-drawers of this kind were characteristic of the grandest furniture of the late 17th century. This piece was made more for display purposes than for any practical use, with very few interior spaces available for storing anything. Oppenordt was of Dutch origin but was working in Paris some time before 1679, when he received letters of naturalisation. He worked for the Gobelins Manufactory and in 1684 was given lodgings in the Louvre; he supplied Louis XIV of France and his court with furniture and marquetry floors. His work often made use of designs by the royal designer Jean Bérain the Elder, which can be detected here in the marquetry.

***The Rainbow Landscape*, about 1636**

Peter Paul Rubens (1577–1640)

H. 137 x W. 233.5 cm | Inv. no. P63

In 1635, the fifty-eight-year-old Rubens bought the country estate of Het Steen, situated between Brussels and Antwerp. Soon afterwards, he painted a view of the house, now in the National Gallery, London, and this companion piece, which shows the surrounding countryside. The two paintings celebrate Rubens's deep love for the landscape of Brabant and are the greatest landscapes he painted. *The Rainbow Landscape*, however, is not a simple naturalistic record. Instead, it is an idealised and symbolic vision of his native landscape. The rainbow recalls the covenant between God and humanity after the Flood and the bountiful harvest associated with peace and prosperity.

Marie de Raet and **Philippe Le Roy,**
1631 and 1630

Anthony van Dyck (1599–1641)
H. 213.3 x W. 114.5 cm | Inv. nos
P79 and P94

Long acknowledged as two of Van Dyck's greatest works
and the finest portraits to survive from his second Antwerp
period (1627–32), these paintings demonstrate the artist's
ability to capture not only his sitters' likenesses but also their
aspirations. Philippe Le Roy was the illegitimate grandson of
a successful Antwerp gunpowder manufacturer. As a result
of his own financial acumen, Philippe, aged only thirty, was
able to acquire the land and feudal rights to the villages of
Ravels and Eel and the right to call himself 'lord of Ravels'.
In 1631, he married Marie de Raet, the sixteen-year-old
daughter of François de Raet, an almoner of Antwerp and
lord of Couwenstyn. He marked this union by commissioning
this pair of portraits from Van Dyck.

This painting depicts the naked figure of Truth being held aloft by her father, Time, who, with his scythe, subdues Falsehood (recognisable by her fine apparel and dissembling mask), while the baleful figure of Discord and Envy recedes, protesting. It demonstrates Lemoyne's ability to combine the compositional models of the 17th century with a more sensual 18th-century tonality. Lemoyne was suffering from severe depression when he was painting this work. The subject may have held a personal significance for the artist: tragically, the day after he completed it, he committed suicide. Yet, as the comte de Caylus, a collector and Lemoyne's biographer, recalled, 'there is no sense of his alienation of spirit in the work, it is even one of his most beautiful cabinet pictures'.

Time saving Truth from Falsehood and Envy,
1737

François Lemoyne (1688–1737)
H. 180.5 x W. 148 cm | Inv. no. P392

St John the Evangelist's Vision of Jerusalem, **1635–8**

Alonso Cano (1601–1667)
H. 82.6 x W. 43.8 cm | Inv. no. P15

According to the Book of Revelation, St John had a vision of a new heaven and a new earth. Here, John kneels before an angel who delicately holds his hand and guides John through his vision. This painting was originally part of a large altarpiece consisting of sculptures and paintings made for the convent of Santa Paula in Seville. The solidity of John and the angel, achieved by Cano's dramatic modelling with light and shadow, might therefore be explained by the presence of actual sculptures nearby. Cano left the project unfinished when he departed for Madrid in 1638.

George IV, 1822

Thomas Lawrence (1769–1830)
H. 270.5 x W. 179 cm | Inv. no. P559

George IV of the United Kingdom was an important figure in the history of the Collection. An avid art collector before he became king in 1820, he was an intimate friend of the 2nd Marchioness of Hertford and on good terms with her son, the future 3rd Marquess of Hertford, who advised him on his purchases and on occasion acted as his saleroom agent. Lawrence, the foremost portraitist of his time and president of the Royal Academy, painted several portraits of the king, though he regarded this as his most successful. A remarkably informal image, it epitomises the elegance and refinement for which George IV was renowned. It was given by the king to his mistress, Lady Conyngham.

The Lady with a Fan, about 1640

Diego Velázquez (1599–1660)
H. 95 x W. 70 cm | Inv. no. P88

The Lady with a Fan is one of Velázquez's most famous paintings, yet the identity of the sitter remains a mystery. Several attempts have been made to identify this enigmatic figure. It has been suggested that she may be either the artist's wife, Juana de Miranda, his daughter, Francisca, or the exiled duchesse de Chevreuse. The closely observed features, penetrating gaze, sober palette and prominently displayed rosary lend the picture an enigmatic aura that has long fascinated viewers. The 19th-century French art historian Théophile Thoré-Bürger claimed that no other painting better represented the art of Velázquez and Spain.

The story of Perseus and Andromeda is told in Ovid's *Metamorphoses*. Andromeda's mother, Queen Cassiopeia, boasted that she and Andromeda were more beautiful than the Nereids, or sea nymphs. Neptune, god of the sea, angry at this insult, sent a sea monster to punish her. Andromeda was chained to a rock as a sacrifice to appease the monster. In Titian's painting, the hero Perseus swoops down to rescue Andromeda, his vertiginous descent contrasting with her passive vulnerability. The painting was part of an important series of six *poesies* (visual poems) painted for Philip II of Spain, a milestone commission in Titian's career.

Perseus and Andromeda, 1554–6

Tiziano Vecellio, called Titian (about 1488/90–1576)

H. 183.3 x W. 199.3 cm | Inv. no. P11

Henri IV, King of France, about 1600

Giovanni da Bologna, called Giambologna (1529–1608)

H. 64.2 cm (without base) | Inv. no. S158

This sculpture depicts Henri IV, the first Bourbon king of France, on horseback and in the guise of a military commander. It is a precursor to the famous equestrian monument of the king installed on the Pont Neuf in Paris in 1614. The statue was destroyed in 1792 during the French Revolution, but a replacement was installed in 1818. Giambologna was fascinated by the horse and thought it an ideal theme for depiction in bronze sculpture. The high point of this preoccupation was his bronze equestrian monument of Cosimo I de' Medici, Grand Duke of Tuscany, which was completed in 1594. There followed a series of further commissions for equestrian monuments from European rulers, including Henri IV.

The Marriage of the Virgin, 1644

Philippe de Champaigne
(1602–1674)
H. 68.8 x W. 141.7 cm | Inv. no. P119

This painting originally formed part of one of the major cycles of paintings commissioned in Paris before the reign of Louis XIV of France. It was painted about 1644 for the oratory of Louis XIII's widow, Anne of Austria, in the Palais-Royal, which she had moved to in 1643. Several leading Parisian painters, including Champaigne, were assigned to depict the life of the Virgin, a fitting subject both for the chapel of a female member of the royal house and for the mother and regent of the future king.

Landscape with Apollo and Mercury, 1660

Claude Gellée, called Claude Lorrain (1604/5(?)–1682)
H. 74.5 x W. 110.4 cm | Inv. no. P114

A melancholy Apollo in the foreground of this painting plays the pipes in memory of his lost love, the nymph Coronis. In the background, Mercury takes advantage of Apollo's absorption to steal away his cattle. The subject, which was used several times by Claude between 1645 and 1666, derives from Ovid's *Metamorphoses*. The true subject of the painting, however, is the luminous morning landscape inspired by the countryside around Rome, which Claude drew and painted throughout his career.

A Dance to the Music of Time, 1634-6

Nicolas Poussin (1594–1665)
H. 82.5 x W. 104 cm | Inv. no. P108

Although Poussin's exquisitely balanced, frieze-like compositions seem antithetical to the notion of movement, the artist actually incorporated representations of dance into many of his paintings. *A Dance to the Music of Time* represents the apogee of this practice. It was made for Giulio Rospigliosi (later Pope Clement IX), who wrote the *libretto* of what may be the first comic opera, and the iconography of dance lies at its very core. In the centre of this painting, a group of figures move gracefully to the music of Father Time. Perhaps they mirror the cycle of the human condition as the laurel-crowned Poverty, the weather-beaten Labour, the sleekly clad Riches and the seductive Pleasure turn in an endless circle. Or perhaps they represent the four seasons, spinning relentlessly.

EAST GALLERY I

DUTCH PAINTINGS: REMBRANDT VAN RIJN AND HIS TIME

Displayed here are paintings by Rembrandt van Rijn, from the painter's early years in Leiden to his later years in Amsterdam, including the moving portrait of his son, Titus. These are combined with a group of Dutch landscapes, from the tonal paintings of Aert van der Neer, to the dramatic vistas of Jacob van Ruisdael and the lush, serene compositions of the latter's pupil, Meindert Hobbema.

The East Galleries were built in 1872–5 to help display the enormous collection, much of which Sir Richard Wallace had inherited from his likely father, the 4th Marquess of Hertford, who had died in 1870. During his lifetime, this gallery housed Wallace's Ottoman, Middle Eastern and Asian arms and armour, which is now displayed on the ground floor.

East Gallery I, about 1888.

Titus, the Artist's Son, **1657**
Rembrandt van Rijn (1606–1669)
H. 68.5 x W. 57.3 cm | Inv. no. P29

Titus was Rembrandt's only surviving child with his first wife, Saskia van Uylenburgh. Soon after their marriage in 1634, the couple began trying to have a family. Sadly, their first three children died in early infancy and Saskia herself died before Titus's first birthday. Titus is shown here at about age sixteen. His serious demeanour might be an allusion to the recent responsibility he was given to manage his father's affairs after the latter had to declare bankruptcy in 1656. Titus wears a 16th-century Venetian costume adorned with a gold earring and chain. His beret beautifully complements the red highlights in his voluminous curls. Rembrandt often dressed up his sitters in various guises. The painting evokes Titus through his likeness but also represents a character created by Rembrandt.

A Winter Scene, **mid-1640s**
Isack van Ostade (1621–1649)
H. 86.4 x W. 107.5 cm | Inv. no. P73

This painting is typical of the atmospheric, silvery-grey winter scenes produced by Van Ostade, in which he successfully marries anecdotal detail with a convincing evocation of the winter landscape. Figures of all ages and from different social classes play and go about their business on the ice. The painting was given to Lady Wallace by Alfred de Rothschild in exchange for another painting by Van Ostade. It was the last work of art to enter the Collection before Lady Wallace's bequest in 1897.

Self-Portrait in a Black Cap, 1637

Rembrandt van Rijn (1606–1669)
H. 63 x W. 50.7 cm | Inv. no. P52

Rembrandt wears a black beret and fur cloak and looks directly towards the viewer. Although now considered to be one of a number of self-portraits Rembrandt painted over the course of his career, its attribution was once questioned due to the uncharacteristic signature, which may have been added by a member of his studio. The portrait is painted on a panel from the same tree used by Rembrandt for another self-portrait from 1634, now in the Gemäldegalerie, Berlin. It is likely that the painting was originally rectangular in shape and later cut down when it was fitted with a frame with a semi-circular top.

***The Listening Housewife (The Eavesdropper),* 1656**

Nicolaes Maes (1634–1693)

H. 84.7 x W. 70.6 cm | Inv. no. P224

The subject of this painting, an eavesdropper exposing the wrongdoings
of other members of a household, is one that Maes favoured. An
elegant housewife smiles coyly as she invites the viewer to witness the
misbehaviour of her servants below stairs. Maes employed a device known
in Dutch as *doorkijkje* (literally 'looking through a door'), which opens the
vista from one room to another offering a glimpse of action beyond the
main scene. Due to the servants' dalliance, a cat licks plates on the kitchen
floor and guests are left unattended in the dining room above. The theme
of admonition is suggested by the painting of Christ at the top left.

A Young Archer, about 1639–40

Govaert Flinck (1615–1660)
H. 66.2 x W. 50.8 cm | Inv. no. P238

A young Black man in a grey-green jacket holds a golden bow in his right hand, while an ornate quiver hangs from his shoulder. His identity is unknown. This painting was most likely not a commissioned portrait but rather a so-called *tronie*, a portrayal of an intriguing individual, often wearing fanciful costume, painted for the open market. Flinck lived and worked in Amsterdam, the Dutch Republic's wealthiest city, which attracted merchants and migrants from all over the Dutch colonies. Flinck studied in Rembrandt van Rijn's studio in the Jodenbreestraat, a neighbourhood where Amsterdam's Black community was concentrated.

A Hermit, about 1661

Gerrit Dou (1613–1675)
H. 32.1 x W. 23.7 cm | Inv. no. P170

A hermit in monkish garb is shown seated in a vaulted interior surrounded by *vanitas* symbols, reminders of the transience of worldly possessions and the inevitability of death. A skull, hourglass and candle recall the brevity and fragility of human life. In contrast, the hermit seeks spiritual solace in the everlasting truths of the Bible open before him. The painting's meticulous finish is typical of Dou's mature style, which inspired the formation of the Leiden school of *fijnschilders* (fine painters), who continued to paint in a similarly polished manner well into the 18th century.

EAST GALLERY II

DUTCH PAINTINGS: GENRE SCENES

Here, the world of the Dutch Republic is explored through small-scale domestic and genre scenes, including masterpieces by Gerard ter Borch, Gabriel Metsu and Jan Steen. Although on the surface most of these paintings depict an orderly and well-mannered society, often they contain hidden meanings, warning their viewers of the temptations and moral traps in this world. There are also outstanding views by Aelbert Cuyp and Jan van der Heyden.

The 3rd Marquess of Hertford's taste for art has been described as his only redeeming feature. He made a number of significant additions to the collection of Dutch and Flemish paintings, favouring the highly finished genre scenes and meticulous townscapes that were fashionable among British collectors in the early 19th century.

East Gallery II, about 1888.

A Woman peeling Apples, 1663

Pieter de Hooch (1629–1684)
H. 67.1 x W. 54.7 cm | Inv. no. P23

De Hooch specialised in domestic genre scenes featuring dramatic perspectival views and sensitivity to natural light. Typical of his carefully composed, light-filled interiors, this painting is a fine example of De Hooch's innovative style. A seated, well-dressed woman peels apples with her child by her side. She represents a positive female role model running a successful household. The complementary theme of marital love is suggested by the Cupid on the fireplace pillar. The painting recalls Johannes Vermeer's paintings of figures in light-filled interiors and was wrongly attributed to him in 1866.

A Lady reading a Letter, about 1665

Gerard ter Borch (1617–1681)
H. 44.2 x W. 32.2 cm | Inv. no. P236

Ter Borch is credited with inventing the high-life interior genre scene, which became popular in the Dutch Republic in the third quarter of the 17th century. A young woman, modelled on Ter Borch's sister, Gesina, sits at a table, its carpet covering pushed aside to allow her to work. Young people reading or writing letters in Dutch paintings of the period are invariably indicators of amorous intrigue. Here, the distracting power of love is suggested by the woman's neglect of her proper household duties. This painting is remarkable for its subtle light and shadow and the artist's confident use of colour.

Celebrating the Birth, **1664**

Jan Steen (1626–1679)

H. 87.7 x W. 107 cm | Inv. no. P111

In this painting, Steen departs from the established tradition of depicting childbirth celebrations, by focusing on the father, rather than the mother, and by suggesting the child's illegitimacy. His subversive treatment of the subject was not apparent until the painting was cleaned in 1983, and the removal of 19th-century paint revealed a hand making the sign of the cuckold above the baby's head. The husband stands at the centre showing off the new child, unaware of the duplicity surrounding him. The cheeky, long-haired man behind the baby is a self-portrait of the artist. To emphasise the husband's impotence, Steen litters the scene with sexual imagery and visual puns.

The Lace Maker,
1662

Caspar Netscher
(1639–1684)
H. 33 x W. 27 cm |
Inv. no. P237

Netscher's undisputed masterpiece, *The Lace Maker* is one of the most successful representations of idealised female virtue in Dutch art. The girl's modest woollen dress implies her lack of vanity, while her absorption in the delicate and difficult task of lace making underlines her seriousness and moral probity. Stylistically, the painting reveals Netscher's sensitivity to the formal experiments of the Delft School, in particular to the understated light-filled interiors of Pieter de Hooch and Johannes Vermeer. The concentrated subject, bold restricted palette and sculptural quality of the figure, offset against a luminous white wall, lend the painting an aura of monumental gravity, belying its modest dimensions.

A Boy bringing Bread, 1663

Pieter de Hooch (1629–1684)
H. 73.5 x W. 59 cm | Inv. no. P27

A boy offers a basket of bread to a woman
in the doorway to a *voorhuis*, the street-
facing room in a Dutch row house. Behind
them, a tiled courtyard leads to a passage,
beyond which a second woman, possibly the
boy's mother, watches the transaction from
across a canal. De Hooch specialised in such
perspectival views through multiple spaces in a
domestic setting, which provide a glimpse into
the private life of prosperous Dutch families in
the 17th century. As in many of his canvases,
the drawn perspective was created by placing
a pin at the vanishing point: the hole can be
detected with the naked eye on the door jamb
at the extreme left of the canvas. The principal
lines of the composition converge on this point.

F414

Pair of corner-cupboards, about 1772

Attributed to Martin Carlin (1730–1785)
H. 97.4 cm | Inv. nos F414–15

The popularity of Boulle-style furniture, typically
veneered in brass and turtleshell, was revived from
about 1760 with the increasing interest in 17th-
century French Classicism and its interpretation
of the antique, and with the so-called Greek taste,
a precursor to the Neoclassical style of the last
quarter of the 18th century. Parisian luxury goods
dealers did much to stimulate this fashion by
selling old pieces by André-Charles Boulle and by
commissioning new pieces in the same manner.
Carlin was a highly accomplished cabinetmaker,
who worked mainly for dealers, but this style of
furniture by him is rare. Boulle-marquetry corner-
cupboards are examples of a furniture type that
appear never to have been made by Boulle himself
in the early 18th century.

Generously sponsored by The Heritage Lottery Fund

EAST GALLERY III

DUTCH PAINTINGS: ITALIANATE PAINTINGS AND SEASCAPES

This gallery includes masterpieces by Nicolaes Berchem, Jan Both, Adriaen van de Velde and Philips Wouwermans. The majority of the paintings are inspired by the light and landscape of Italy, whether the artist actually visited Italy or not. Their warm light effects and elegance are echoed in the highly finished, classicising paintings by Jan and Willem van Mieris and Adriaen van der Werff.

East Galleries II and III formed a single top-lit picture gallery in Sir Richard and Lady Wallace's lifetime. Known as the Modern Gallery, it housed most of the 19th-century paintings in the Collection, as well as many of the smaller-scale medieval and Renaissance sculptures and works of art.

East Gallery III, about 1888.

The Migration of Jacob, 1663

Adriaen van de Velde (1636–1672)
H. 133.5 x W. 180 cm | Inv. no. P80

The subject of this painting is taken from the Old Testament and represents Jacob's flight from his father-in-law, Laban, with his wives, possessions and cattle. In this highly original composition, Jacob and his family form a procession that undulates across the landscape. Light is cast on the central figures, while others further back are cast in shadow. The dark, brooding clouds overhead add a sense of urgency to their journey. Van de Velde came from a family of painters; his father and brother worked in the marine genre, while he specialised in landscapes. Van de Velde was a particularly gifted draughtsman, equally skilled in depicting figures and animals, and was often called upon to paint figures into landscapes by other artists.

Italian Landscape, **probably about 1645–52**

Jan Both (about 1618–1652)
H. 81.2 x W. 104.7 cm | Inv. no. P28

Both worked in Rome with his brother, Andries, between 1638–41. While there, he collaborated with the landscape painter Claude Gellée, called Claude Lorrain, from whom he adopted the method of arranging his compositions along diagonal lines to achieve greater recession into depth, as well as the method of unifying his landscapes with a golden light. He was extremely prolific, and his decorative landscapes were popular in the 18th and early 19th centuries. This picture is painted on a brownish ground, typical of Both's landscapes produced shortly after his return from Italy in 1641. It represents a mountainous country, divided by a winding road on which two travellers halt to speak to a peasant. On the left is a herdsman with two goats.

Table, 1785

Attributed to François Rémond (1747–1812)
H. 82 cm | Inv. no. F317

This table was almost certainly made under the direction of a well-known Parisian luxury goods dealer, Dominique Daguerre, and executed by the bronzeworker Rémond, one of the most skilful gilders in Paris. The delicate frieze mounts feature many attributes of Bacchus, the god of wine, which were typical of the Neoclassical taste of late 18th-century France. The most striking aspect of the table are the beautiful female figures that support the four corners, dressed in classical robes and protected by tasselled cushions on their heads. These are of an exceptional quality rarely matched in gilt bronze. They echo the statues on the Erectheion in Athens.

A Coast Scene with Classical Ruins, 1649

Jan Baptist Weenix (1621–1660)
H. 82 x W. 107.5 cm | Inv. no. P117

Weenix was born in Amsterdam but studied in Rome. He led the way in developing the harbour scene as a pictorial genre in the Dutch Republic. This imaginary coastal scene is considered to be one of his finest works. An Italianate setting is suggested by Corinthian columns, a porphyry tomb (copied from one that then stood before the Pantheon in Rome) and a pyramid (evoking the tomb of Cestius near the Porta Ostiensis in Rome). The motif of the couple dallying before antique ruins may be intended to warn the viewer that love does not last forever.

A Southern Harbour Scene, late 1650s

Nicolaes Berchem (1620–1683)
H. 82.9 x W. 103.7 cm | Inv. no. P25

Typical of Berchem's decorative and exotic harbour scenes, the harbour was imaginatively identified with the port of Genoa by Jacques Aliamet, who engraved the painting in the 18th century. The painting's distinguished provenance demonstrates the artist's appeal to collectors in the 18th and 19th centuries. Its owners included the duc de Berry and Anatole Demidoff, Prince of San Donato. The 4th Marquess of Hertford paid the considerable price of 42,000 francs (about £1,680) for the painting at the latter's sale in 1868.

The Horse Fair, late 1660s

Philips Wouwermans (1619–1668)
H. 64.3 x W. 88.4 cm | Inv. no. P65

The Horse Fair is the most famous of the paintings by Wouwermans in the Collection. It demonstrates Wouwermans's strengths as a landscapist in creating subtle evocations of a vaguely Mediterranean or Italianate terrain and atmosphere. The technical virtuosity of the handling and the painting's decorative quality won it great renown in 18th-century France. One commentator wrote: 'No picture by Wouwermans surpasses this in its fine touch, fresh colouring and brilliance, which exceed the imagination'. Such elegant subjects, often bearing distinguished provenances, endeared Wouwermans's works to the 4th Marquess of Hertford, who bought at least seven paintings by the artist.

EAST DRAWING ROOM

PAINTING IN 17TH-CENTURY ANTWERP AND BRUSSELS

With the exception of Michael Sweerts, the painters represented in this room are closely associated with Antwerp, where they trained. Anthony van Dyck, Peter Paul Rubens and David Teniers the Younger also served as court painters to the archducal court at Brussels. Most of these artists worked for an international clientele and some, like Van Dyck and Rubens, spent long periods abroad. Teniers's small copies after Italian masters in the collection of Archduke Leopold Wilhelm of Austria in Brussels reflect the importance of Italian art in the Netherlands.

In the first decades of the 19th century, the East Drawing Room was the 2nd Marchioness of Hertford's sitting room. Here, she entertained the Prince Regent during his daily visits, which lasted throughout their friendship, from 1806 until his accession as George IV of the United Kingdom in 1820. At the time, the room was furnished with salmon-coloured silk curtains, white and gold seat furniture and the marchioness's collection of Sèvres porcelain.

The East Drawing Room, about 1888.

These three preparatory sketches relate to Rubens's intended cycle illustrating the life of Henri IV of France, destined for the Luxembourg Palace in Paris. The series of twenty-four paintings, depicting the battles, combats, conquests and triumphs of Henri IV 'in the manner of the triumphs of the Romans', as specified in the contract signed by Rubens in 1622, was commissioned by his wife, Marie de' Medici, and intended to complement a similar series that showed her own 'illustrious life and heroic acts'. Rubens completed the sketches for the second set in 1628. He never completed the final paintings, progress for which was hampered by disputes concerning their size and finally halted by the enforced exile of his patron in 1631.

The Birth of Henri IV, The Triumph of Henri IV and *The Union of Henri IV and Marie de Médicis*, **1628**

Peter Paul Rubens (1577–1640)
H. 21.5 x W. 37.2 cm (P522), H. 21.2 x W. 9.9 cm (P523) and
H. 23 x W. 12.2 cm (P524) | Inv. nos P523, P522 and P524

Charles I, King of England, 1759
Louis François Roubiliac (1695–1762)
H. 71 cm | Inv. no. S23

In 1636, Gian Lorenzo Bernini, the Italian master of baroque sculpture, made a celebrated bust of Charles I of England. The bust, modelled after portraits painted by Anthony van Dyck, was lost in a fire at the Palace of Whitehall in 1698, but it continued to inspire sculptors long into the 18th century. This bust is a free interpretation of Bernini's sculpture by Roubiliac, a French sculptor who spent much of his career in England. It was made for Matson House, the home of politician George Augustus Selwyn. Charles I lodged there in 1643 during the Siege of Gloucester – an episode of the English Civil War (1642–51). Selwyn bequeathed the bust to his adopted daughter, later the 3rd Marchioness of Hertford.

Console table, about 1705
Attributed to André-Charles Boulle
(1642–1732)
H. 100 cm | Inv. no. F56

Of a radical and innovative design, this table amply shows the creative genius of Boulle. It is possible that, with its paw feet and lion mask, it was a model of a table Boulle made for the use of the wife of Louis XIV of France's grandson, the young duchesse de Bourgogne. In 1701, she was given an apartment at the zoo in the gardens of the Palace of Versailles, called the Château de Ménagerie, for her entertainment, and Boulle supplied seven tables with animal-themed decoration. Such a table would be fitted against a wall, typically between two windows. The table surface is of Boulle marquetry, which makes it very delicate and less practical than a marble top.

A Riverside Inn, about **1645–50**

David Teniers the Younger (1610–1690)
H. 22.8 x W. 34.5 cm | Inv. no. P196

In the 1640s and 1650s, Teniers's style changed as he began to paint open-air peasant scenes, many set in front of an inn and executed in a varied and colourful palette, often comprising an idyllic element. In 1637, he married the daughter of the painter Jan Bruegel the Elder, and a subsequent series of public appointments indicate his increasing social prominence. In 1651, he became court painter to Archduke Leopold Wilhelm of Austria and moved to Brussels. Such brightly coloured, idealised views were in keeping with the tastes of the fashionable elite for whom Teniers worked. This painting was referred to as 'The Diamond' in the 19th century, owing to its fresh, jewel-like execution.

An Allegory of Fruitfulness, **1620–29**

Jacob Jordaens (1593–1678)

H. 200.7 x W. 229 cm | Inv. no. P120

In this unusual and enigmatic composition, a group of satyrs and humans of various ages are gathered around a woman, who holds a large cornucopia. The grapes proffered by other figures invoke the hedonistic world of the wine god Bacchus, who, according to ancient Roman mythology, presides over the autumn harvest. The central figure points to two children, leaving us in no doubt that this is a celebration of Nature's bounty. Jordaens probably did not have a single literary source in mind but rather intended to draw out the close association of peace and fecundity, particularly at a time when the war-torn Netherlands was enjoying a period of peace (known as the Twelve Years' Truce).

A Boor Asleep, **1630s**

Adriaen Brouwer (about 1605/6–1638)

H. 36.6 x W. 27.6 cm | Inv. no. P211

The delicate palette and brilliant handling of this exquisite example of Brouwer's art, painted on a beige ground, are typical of the artist's maturity and help explain his appeal to contemporaries, such as Rembrandt van Rijn and Peter Paul Rubens. The composition was popular and frequently copied, Brouwer himself producing a number of closely related compositions. When the German art historian Gustav Friedrich Waagen saw *A Boor Asleep* at Hertford House in 1854, he described it as 'by far the finest example of this rare master I know'.

GLOSSARY

ACANTHUS
A stylised leaf of the *acanthus spinosus* plant.

ARABESQUE
Decoration based on rhythmic linear patterns of scrolling and interlacing foliage and tendrils.

BURNISHING
The process of rubbing metal to a sheen.

CASTING
The process of pouring metal into moulds; also called **Founding**.

CHASING
The finishing of a cast metal surface with chisels and files.

CHINOISERIE
A Western imitation or evocation of East Asian art or culture, often through highly stylised motifs.

COMMEDIA DELL'ARTE
A type of improvised theatre, originating in Italy, with a cast of lively characters.

CRUCIBLE STEEL
A type of steel made by melting steel and other materials in a crucible.

EARTHENWARE
A type of porous ceramic made from clay fired at low temperatures.

EMBOSSING
The process of applying relief decoration to materials.

ETCHING
The process of using acids to incise designs into materials.

FANCY PICTURE
A type of painting, usually of a single figure, that borrows from portraiture conventions but depicts an anonymous model.

FÊTE GALANTE
A type of painting showing idealised scenes of elegant people in the countryside.

GENRE PAINTING
A type of painting depicting scenes from daily life.

GILDING
The process of applying gold to a surface.

GILT BRONZE
Metal, typically brass, rather than bronze, that has been gilded using an amalgam of mercury and gold; see *Gilding*.

GOBELINS MANUFACTORY
The factory established on behalf of the French crown in 1664, which produced works of art for royal residences. After 1699, the factory produced tapestries exclusively.

GROTESQUE
A fanciful type of ornament derived from ancient Roman interior decoration rediscovered during the Renaissance.

GROUND
A background to which paint or decoration is applied.

HARD-PASTE PORCELAIN
A translucent type of porcelain containing kaolin, quartz and feldspar, which is more easily worked than soft-paste porcelain and can withstand higher temperatures; see *Soft-paste porcelain*.

HEAT BLUEING
The process of heating a polished steel surface to give it a decorative and protective layer of blue oxidisation.

HISTORY PAINTING
A type of painting depicting classical, biblical or mythological subjects.

LACQUER
A waterproof varnish produced by tapping the sap of the *rhus vernicifera* tree and applying it to wood, fabric and other materials.

MAIOLICA
Italian tin-glazed earthenware; see *Earthenware*.

MARQUETRY
A type of veneer in which shaped pieces of wood and other materials are combined to form a design and then glued to a surface. **Boulle marquetry** typically consists of turtleshell and brass.

PARIS SALON
An exhibition held by the Royal Academy of Painting and Sculpture in the 18th century, and by the Academy of Fine Arts in the 19th century.

SÈVRES MANUFACTORY
The French porcelain factory established in about 1740, which became a royal enterprise when bought by Louis XV of France in 1759.

SOFT-PASTE PORCELAIN
An artificial type of porcelain made without kaolin, which is more opaque than hard-paste porcelain and less able to withstand high temperatures; see *Hard-paste porcelain*.

STRAPWORK
Geometric decoration of stylised leather straps.

TURQUERIE
A Western imitation or evocation of Ottoman art or culture, often through highly stylised motifs.